D1263992

ENCORES ON MAIN STREET

AUTHORIZED DISTRIBUTING AGENT
RUTGERS UNIVERSITY PRESS
NEW BRUNSWICK, NEW JERSEY

Encores

ON MAIN STREET

Successful Community Theatre

Leadership

By

TALBOT PEARSON

CARNEGIE INSTITUTE OF TECHNOLOGY PRESS

PITTSBURGH 1948

COPYRIGHT 1948 BY
THE CARNEGIE INSTITUTE OF TECHNOLOGY PRESS
IN PITTSBURGH, PENNSYLVANIA

The author and publishers wish to thank the following authors and their publishers for their kind permission to use material in this book.

Harcourt, Brace and Company, Inc., for material from Norris
Houghton's *Advance from Broadway*, and from Kenneth Mac-
Gowan's *Footlights Across America*; Pitman Publishing Com-
pany for excerpts from *Curtain's Going Up* by Albert McCleary
and Carl Glick, and *The Amateur Theatrical Handbook* by
Harold Markham; and Charles Scribner's Sons for material
from *The Flower in Drama* and *Theatre Practice* by Stark
Young.

PRINTED IN THE UNITED STATES OF AMERICA

792
P362

PN 3155
.P43

Foreword

〰〰〰〰〰〰〰〰〰〰〰〰〰〰〰〰〰〰〰〰〰〰〰〰〰〰〰〰〰〰〰〰〰〰

THE original undertaking of this book was made possible by a generous grant-in-aid from the National Theatre Conference. I am especially grateful, therefore, to Sawyer Falk, Frederic McConnell, and Barclay S. Leathem, the officers of the Conference, for their practical encouragement and their expressed belief that my experiences and conclusions might have some value for younger practitioners.

My thanks go, also, to Elise McGehee for wise counsel on the approach; to Carl Glick, for help on a multitude of details; to Harold Helvenston for his apt illustrations; to John Rosenfield for support and encouragement through the years, and to him and Peggy-Louise Jones for a tedious job of research; and to my wife for never-failing comradeship, and affection sorely tried, during the production of nearly two hundred plays.

I pay tribute, further, to all those theatre enthusiasts in Dallas, Memphis, Santa Barbara, Shreveport, and Youngstown who have unwittingly provided the material for this chronicle, and to my students in the Carnegie Department of Drama who have heard me with attentive patience.

JUN 4 1954

Foreword

To the members of the book committee of Carnegie Institute of Technology Press, who have paid me the compliment of selecting this work as the first to be published under the Carnegie imprint, I am indebted for a unique opportunity.

TALBOT PEARSON

October, 1947

Contents

wwwwwwwwwwwwwwwwwwwwwwwwwwwwwwwwwwwwwwwwwwwwwwwwwwwwwwwwwwwwwwwwwwwwwwwwwwwwww

of questions—desirability of organized interrogation—
frankness on both sides—exploring all avenues—hedging to be avoided—trustees' opinion the only important
one—irresponsible contacts dangerous—full discussion
of policy and program—virtue of accurate reporting—
dangers of impetuosity—value of calm reflection—
caution before final decision enjoined upon both parties.

Contents

confidence between director and president—proper appreciation of volunteer efforts—contributions not in line of duty—middle path between neglect and adulation—production staff preferable to committee—who makes the appointments?—staff plan of operations—the timetable—vital co-ordination—difficulties of terminology—need for semantics—misunderstandings from lack of comprehension—rejecting the unwanted contribution—the ideal committee.

ENCORES ON MAIN STREET

CHAPTER ONE

"A Little Work, A Little Play . . ."

THE TERM "COMMUNITY THEATRE" IS USED TO COVER ALL THOSE
play-producing groups which operate in the United States of
America under a wide variety of names—little theatre, civic
playhouse, community theatre, community playhouse and a
dozen or more variants and combinations. There is nothing
standardized about either the titles or operations of these
groups; they show no sign of regimentation in either their
tactics or their strategy and they pay no dues to a central organization. They are no more than an agglomeration of highly
individual civic associations, bound together by a general simi-
larity of motives and ideals.

The participants in these community endeavors are amateurs
and their avocation is dramatics, but standards of operation
are, in the main, as far removed from the "amateur dramatics"
of an earlier generation as a technicolor movie is from a Mack
Sennett comedy. These citizens pursue their avocation in an
age where a high standard of competence in the parallel professional entertainment fields—Broadway, radio, movies—has
made it necessary for the nonprofessional in the theatre to
learn his craft thoroughly and practise it conscientiously in
order to find and retain an audience. The community theatre

is not big business but it is now, if never before, a very serious
business.

The well-established regional theatres are now playing to the
largest audiences in their history. It is approximately twenty-
five years since the major groups began their operations and
most of them appeared to have reached the peak of their effec-
tiveness around 1929. The subsequent depression made severe
test of their vitality and staying power; many groups, conceived
in optimism and dedicated to the economic philosophy of the
Coolidge era, had painful experiences with their mortgage-
holders, several theatres gave up the fight altogether, and the
survivors played to dwindling audiences and were compelled
to curtail their operations quite drastically. Some groups even
compromised with their ideals and made pathetic and even
ludicrous efforts to pay the bills and keep the doors open.
Sponsorship of circus performances, raffles for automobiles,
white elephant sales, and bingo games were among the many
devices used to augment the meager box-office receipts. Such
eccentricities are no longer necessary; the box-office pays the
bills nowadays, with something over.

In the lush days prior to 1929 some of us with a passion for
statistics used to calculate that the saturation point had been
reached when an audience (for each production) which averaged 3 percent of the city's population could be counted on.
Many theatres managed very well by attracting only half that
figure; any higher percentage was regarded as phenomenal,
therefore rare and perhaps incredible.

The statistics for today's audiences would indeed seem incredible to some of the pioneers, for there are a dozen or more
nonprofessional theatres currently showing their productions
to more than 7 percent of their community's population. In
the season of 1945–1946 at least one theatre sold 5,400 subscription tickets, which represented almost 9 percent of the
63,000 available ticket-buyers. As this latter figure was supplied by the local chamber of commerce, it is fair to assume
that the potential was not an understatement. This theatre is

an exceptional case, for it enjoys great prestige and supplies the needs of a community which is off the track of the bigger road companies. There are, however, many community groups who are regularly attracting 5 or 6 percent of the total number of their fellow citizens without claiming anything phenomenal for their operations.

No exact figures are available on the total number of non-professional groups at present in active operation. A leading play-agent in the country has estimated that his New York office rents (that is, collects the royalty legally due him as agent for the author) at least one play a year to each of over 20,000 dramatic organizations, and other publishers may well be able to say the same. Included in these figures, of course, will be every conceivable variety of dramatic venture, ranging all the way from a campfire presentation by a boy-scout troop to a production, in full panoply, by the Pasadena Playhouse. The scouts will forgive me, I trust, for putting them at the foot of the scale, the reason being that their plays are frequently given for an audience restricted to the other members of their troop, and not for the general public. At the same time, it may be unjust to select the Pasadena theatre as an appropriate contrast, since there are many other groups in the country who attract even larger houses for their plays. But the well-deserved renown of the California organization justifies the use of its name, since it is certainly the best known of the larger community theatres.

At the present time there are probably between nine hundred and a thousand active producing groups other than colleges and high schools. Of these, some three hundred either own their own buildings or occupy quarters which afford them adequate facilities and give them a feeling of permanence and continuity. Practically all these three hundred theatres employ professional directors on a full-time basis. Some of the larger theatres find it necessary and desirable to engage, in addition, such functionaries as an assistant director, a technical director, a wardrobe mistress, and so on, in order to keep up their production schedule and to free the nonprofessional participants for the business of acting. In every group there are, fortunately, a goodly number of amiable persons who have no acting ambitions and who prefer to contribute their time and talent to the purely technical side of production. Such people are invaluable, and without their help the professional staff would never get the curtain up on time. There is much more to the "putting on" of a play than is dreamed of in the average actor's philosophy.

The purpose of this book, the writing of which was made possible by a generous grant from the National Theatre Conference, is to present a discussion of the relationship which should exist between the community theatre director and the people with whom he has to work. These latter include the players, the technicians, the committees, the audience, and, most important of all, the trustees to whom he is responsible and whose approval of his efforts is essential to his continued working existence. All these people, the trustees in particular, are amateurs. To them the theatre is merely an avocation, a spare-time exercise, and a source of mental, physical, and even spiritual refreshment. The director is a professional whose happiness, security, and freedom of expression depend upon the success with which he can harness their efforts, maintain their enthusiasm, and retain their respect and confidence.

Although addressed primarily to the director because the burden of adjustment lies principally with him (or her), these chapters may possibly be helpful to other active workers in the community theatre. This is not a textbook on the art of directing or scene design. It is not a handbook of general theatre procedure. There is a large number of such books already available. Competent authorities have written exhaustively on the technical side of theatre production, on the planning and conduct of rehearsals, and on the art of blending the various contributing elements into an aesthetically satisfying unity. Whether it be regarded as art or science the practice of theatre production may be studied, if not entirely mastered, by means of the already existing literature on the subject.

None of these admirable textbooks completely fill the director's need for guidance because they tend to presuppose ideal working conditions, which simply do not exist in the community theatre. The writers of these books take for granted a near-Utopian standard of competence on the part of the players, complete and efficient co-operation from the assisting staff (presumably highly trained and professional), and the consistently maintained support of the producing authority. There can be no quarrel with this approach. It is only correct to presume the existence of perfect conditions if a perfect result is to be secured. In the compilation of a treatise on the practice of an art it is only proper to presuppose that all the tools and materials will be of the highest obtainable quality if the finest results are to be obtained.

The object of this book is not to advocate lower standards nor to excuse poor workmanship, but to attempt a more realistic attitude which will at the same time be consonant with high ideals and sincere effort. There is no real escape from the imperfections of this world, even in the theatre. Human beings are never so difficult as when engaged in an avocation, and diverse personalities are never so conflicting as in the glare of the spotlights, where self-expression is apotheosized and inhibition is condemned.

Not all the graduates of our drama schools and college theatres have their eyes on a Broadway career. Their teachers will have done their best to discourage a dip into that pool of heartbreak and disillusionment for all but the hardiest swimmers, but there will always be plenty of courageous young people disregarding all warnings in their anxiety to take a chance at the glittering prizes offered by Broadway and Hollywood. At the same time there are many of equal talent and courage who deliberately decline the exhausting experience of spending their postgraduate years shuttling back and forth

through Shubert Alley in search of their first job. It is quite
unfair to condemn as lacking in courage these young actors
and actresses, these embryo directors and scene designers who
choose to find their careers and their self-expression in the
greater theatre away from Broadway.

Unfortunately far too many of this latter group start out
with rosy visions of the temple of Thespis at whose altars they
will serve reverently and joyously. They have learned their craft
under the happiest of circumstances, in schools where harmony
and co-operation among students and faculty were taken for
granted, where costumes were always authentic, settings complete down to the last gilt doorknob, and where the dictates of
the rehearsal call board were final and absolute. In short they
have been reared in the proper theatre atmosphere and under
circumstances calculated to imbue them with the highest possible standards and ideals.

Actual conditions of work in the majority of community
theatres are vastly different and often most disillusioning.
Many brilliant young theatre people, whose talents should
have been available to the larger American theatre, have been
so dismayed by their first experience of the provincial drama
that they have worked out their first contract and then de-
parted into other fields. I am not arguing that they should have
stayed on at the price of a compromise with their standards,
but that some fuller understanding of the special problems of
the nonprofessional theatre would have enabled them to ad-
just to conditions and methods foreign to their training.

There are some powerful and successful community theatres
in the country whose organization and production methods
leave little to be desired. They are professional in the best sense
of that word, but their competence has been achieved as a
result of careful planning and wise leadership over a period of
time. Such theatres, it must be admitted, are the exception and
not the rule. These highly competent groups have been fortunate in the loyal citizens who have devoted time and thought

to their problems and maintained their support through trying times. They have been fortunate, also, in their professional leaders who have occupied their posts for many years and who have arrived at a philosophy and a technique in their human relationships.

The others, which means practically all of them, have a less settled policy and seem to prefer to experiment quite freely. Many of them subscribe to the theory that a director should move around, much in the same way that the ministers of the Methodist Church revolve in their pastorates. In many cities this practice seems to have proved successful, and it has much to recommend it, but unless a policy of this kind, and the reason for it, are properly understood by the trustees, the director, and the public, it is apt to lead to hardship, if not to hard feelings.

Since every city has an individuality and every board of trustees conceives its responsibility to the membership and the audience differently, it is immediately obvious that no yardstick can be supplied to any given circumstances. These discussions must view the problems in the broadest terms.

The author, after nearly twenty-five years of active work in this field, looks back upon many errors of omission and commission. There were situations and problems which might have been handled better. Viewed objectively, the mistakes shine out with a blinding glare and difficulties which at the time seemed insuperable appear, at this safe distance, the merest molehills.

In extenuation it should be remembered that when the Dallas Little Theatre, later to become perhaps the outstanding theatre of its kind in the country, was founded, it was a shot in the dark for everyone concerned. Nothing like it had been attempted before and there were no textbooks on the subject. It was a combination of theatre and social relations, of practical business and community culture. The director was teacher, football coach, and cheerleader, yet few of the first groups organized could see in his work the necessity for full-time employment. The ball was fumbled rather frequently by all in those days, and the lessons were learned the hard way.

It is from such mistakes, sometimes repeated in later years, that profit can be derived. At the same time, immodesty compels the complacent admission that some situations were handled well and with constructive results, which may appear in the ensuing chapters.

From these years of active experience, from miscalculations or from the successful outcome of thoughtful planning and approach, there may evolve some pattern by which the professional may live happily and successfully among the earnest people who find their avocation in the theatre. Since the science of directing has been reduced to terms, perhaps by similar ratiocination the art of theatre leadership may eventually be expressed in a form which will prevent broken hearts and spirits, will offer constructive suggestions for more felicitous relations and help to carry the greater American theatre to larger achievement.

This little volume cannot hope to supply all the answers, but its contribution may not be too inconsiderable. It is largely a record of facts, relieved only occasionally by suggestions for some techniques which, in my opinion, could be improved. Included in the facts are a number of incidents, unadorned and devoid of exaggeration, of a personal nature. I have avoided the mention of actual names, for obvious reasons, but since I recall none of these happenings with any bitterness and repeat them without malicious intent, I trust that if the persons concerned recognize themselves they will find pleasure in reliving with me the days when we worked, suffered, and rejoiced together.

CHAPTER TWO

The Goldfish Bowl

A LEADER WHO POSSESSES COURAGE AND CONVICTION NEVER LACKS followers. Every community theatre must depend, for the regular presentation of its yearly program, upon the volunteer efforts of at least a couple of hundred persons who are willing followers of a trusted leader. Many theatres are able to make use of the time and talents of as many as five hundred workers, for besides the actors and actresses who make up the casts there will be those who work behind the scenes, in the front of the house, and on committees or membership campaigns and publicity ventures. All these genuine amateurs, lovers of the theatre, have to be continually and continuously inspired by the chosen leader, the director.

Like the proverbial teacher who has always to be one day ahead of her pupils, the theatre leader has to be, in fervor and zeal, always one jump ahead of his volunteer helpers. He must be able to maintain a constant stream of enthusiasm and encouragement, to have on tap a solution for every difficulty, and to meet every setback with a smile. This outpouring of spirit is likely to prove wearing and depleting, and it leaves little or no time for creative work in playwriting or the compilation of textbooks.

In the same way that many ministers of religion are prevented from doing the research and study necessary to produce

There is no escape from this

their best sermons by the multitudinous demands on their time as parish executives, many theatre leaders are unsuccessful in being director, manager, organizer, and publicist all rolled into one. But these duties are only part of those expected from a community theatre leader, and they are inseparable from the job. The challenge must be accepted and the problem must be faced with a good heart.

The first few months of a director's term of office are occupied largely by the business of correlating the energies of the individuals who adhere to the community group. Not that this phase of the leader's job is ever finished, but the first few months are of vital importance. There will be no privacy. A constant stream of visitors will be the rule. Ostensibly they will come to see if there is anything they can be given to do, to offer good wishes, often to enlarge upon the shortcomings of the predecessor, but actually they are busy sizing up the new incumbent and trying to discover what makes him (or her) tick. After they leave the theatre they will probably make a dash for the nearest telephone booth to report their findings to their familiars. Fortified by this information the next visitors will arrive, gossip a while and then go on their way to pass along the good word—or the bad—to another circle of friends.

There is no escape from this, irritating and even fearsome as it may sound in prospect. Every young minister knows about it; so does his wife, and if the theatre director is fortunate enough to be married then he and his partner must resign themselves to living like goldfish as long as they stay in this profession. After all, they are on the inside looking out, which is occasionally an advantage, and that point of view can provide much amusement for theatre directors as well as for goldfish. If the director has a genuine love of people, as he must have if he is to succeed in this work, he will enjoy the visits of these sight-seers and make capital out of the time spent in contact with them.

The ability to be a good listener is essential. These early callers may be depended on to make most of the conversation.

They will voice their complaints, offer their suggestions, and expect to be heard and to have their ideas seriously considered. It is not wise for the new director to offer them too much encouragement. He may expect to be quoted and, at that, not too accurately. Any rash promises as to policy are unsafe; after all, policy in general is the province of the trustees. It may be prompted by the suggestions of the director, indeed some recommendations as to change or modification will be expected from him, but they should not be publicly stated until the trustees have heard about them. In that way lies trouble of the worst kind. The director should always remember he is the executive, not the legislature. His duties are concerned with tactics whereas strategy is determined by the trustees.

The director's visitors may make the mistake of deciding for or against him on the basis of the first interchange of views and news. Most of them do, which is why the new appointee must be at his best. But he should not make a similar error himself. It is all too easy to put people immediately into pigeonholes or neatly package them under type this or that, pleasant or unpleasant, trustworthy or otherwise. The director will be expected to be at his best and most charming, while the visitor may make no attempt to put himself out to please, may even be masochistic enough to put his worst side forward in order to see how it is taken. Early generalizations on the director's part are fatal in this business of rallying support for an enterprise which draws its personnel and its audience from every stratum of the city's life, which includes in its repertory everything from *Three Sisters* to *Three Men on a Horse* and which must needs enrapture the Browning Club one week and the Rotary Club the next. All kinds of people make up the audience but a far more diversified collection of human beings seek active self-expression in the practical work of the theatre.

Away from the theatre, on neutral ground elsewhere in the city, the danger of generalization is even greater. It is sometimes permissible to cast for type on the stage, but never in public contacts. The man or woman who is "just crazy about the theatre" and who goes to New York twice a year for the express purpose of seeing the latest plays would seem to be a reliable confidant to whom the director could pour out his plans and his dreams, while the hardheaded man of business, whose only publicized associations are in luncheon clubs or sporting circles, might be hurriedly classified as a philistine and given scant consideration. This is a dangerous fallacy. Many of these businessmen "types" have been revealed as secret collectors of classical recordings or as ardent lovers of Shakespeare, which they read in bed. A man of this kind may be found more willing to encourage and support a local enterprise than the one who disparages his own city's efforts towards "the better life" and believes that Broadway, and only Broadway, contains the ark of the theatrical covenant.

The director must then be patient and eternally curious, with always a genuine respect for his chosen profession and a love for his work that he can carry around with him like a banner. "Take your job very seriously, but take yourself very lightly" should be the watchword. A community theatre director has nothing to apologize for in his position as the leader of a worthy and valuable civic cause, but he must speak always for his theatre, not for himself. He should learn to say "we" and not "I."

The reasons for this becoming modesty are quite logical. It must be remembered that the longer a community group has been in existence the greater is the pride of ownership exhibited by those who serve as its trustees and take part in its activities. Many groups of twenty-five years active existence still include men and women who were charter members of the organization, and some of these people have even served continuously on the governing board.

Whether or not this long service is a healthy situation is not the point under discussion. If the group has retained such people in office, it must have been because of some great value placed upon their services or their opinions, and such men and women will still be active in the making of the theatre's policy.

If their views on the objectives of the group should happen to coincide with the director's they will be his warm friends; if not, they are likely to prove quite dangerous foes. This possibility must be faced and, at least in the early stages, any open conflict of opinion on policy and procedure quite sedulously avoided. There are many ways in which these elder statesmen can, and will, help the incoming director, for their background of local history will be unexcelled. It will usually be found that over the years they have given more than mere lip service to the cause. If they have not made large donations of money, they have probably been generous with their time and effort. It is *their* theatre, because they have nursed and helped rear it to maturity.

Succeeding chapters will endeavor to analyze the particular problems confronting the director in his contact with the veteran trustees and workers, and with all the different groups around the theatre. Suggestions will be advanced as to ways and means to meet and overcome difficulties which may arise in the various departments. Even if the proposed solutions were infallible, and I should be the last to claim that they are, they will be useless without certain personal qualities that the director himself must bring to the task.

There was an old Victorian couplet, designed to point a moral, which ran something like this:

> "Patience and Perseverance
> Made a bishop of His Reverence."

Patience and perseverance are still useful qualities, even outside the ecclesiastical hierarchy; so are control of the temper, unfailing tact, and a becoming modesty about one's ability to judge human nature correctly. It may be remembered that even psychiatrists have been known to disagree. Rash judgments are extremely risky and it is much safer to give everyone the benefit of the doubt. Things have a way of straightening themselves out—if left alone—that is positively uncanny. There will be countless surprises, most of them pleasant, because people will not stay classified, the director least of all. In spite of a careful guard on his temper and his tongue, he may frequently be misjudged by his fellow workers. Therefore he should avoid a snap judgment or a rash estimate of character which may land him in an untenable position, weaken his authority, and lead to unhappiness all round.

However platitudinous the foregoing suggestions may sound they are the basic rules of behavior from which must be developed the special techniques for each particular case. There is no denying that a severe self-discipline is called for, a constant vigilance and a stern resolve to make things come out right in the face of setbacks and opposition. Much can be achieved by arranging the work schedule so as to provide the proper amount of rest and preparation for the strain of rehearsal and committee work. There is no point in subjecting the nervous system to fatigue which could be avoided by a little thought and planning.

Careful organizing of the day's activities is essential. In the preoccupation with committee work, social contacts, office routine, and general supervision, many directors tend to lose sight of the fact that their principal contribution must be the rehearsal and production of plays. Upon the well-ordered conduct of rehearsals depends the success of the theatre under their charge. Everything else is of secondary importance. A play without lights, scenery, or costumes is still a play if it is properly acted; no amount of elaborate scenic investiture, no miracles of lighting will make a play if the cast is unprepared and low in its morale.

It is therefore a mistake to keep open house, to be at the disposal of every chance caller until such a late hour as makes it impossible to eat a proper meal before rehearsal. A hastily swallowed sandwich is not adequate fortification for three, four, or five hours of intense nervous concentration. Nor is a dinner party, preceded by cocktails and possibly garnished with other forms of firewater, any better. The players, who may themselves have had no more than a sandwich in order to be on time, will not welcome the ministrations of a director who is either somnolent from rich food or exuberant from the other concomitants of a festive occasion. Dining out is delightful, and it is a desirable form of recreation and refreshment for the director, but invitations had better be accepted for evenings when there is no rehearsal.

The conduct of rehearsals, the guidance, teaching, and encouragement of nonprofessionals, who often make great sacrifices of time, energy, and convenience in order to take part in plays, is the director's foremost duty. He should come to rehearsals as nearly as possible in peak condition, mental and physical. To be exhausted or distraught, hungry or surfeited, is to break faith with his fellow workers. He must therefore learn to say no, to plan his days so that his own social life does not impinge upon the principal hours of his theatre schedule, to organize his time so that there is always a space in which he can take some rest, away from the theatre, for an hour or more before the time to meet his cast.

This is a prescription acquired from bitter experience. It is a good thing to be known as a social animal, to have the reputation of being able to take long hours and yet be on hand to meet people at any and all times. It is dangerous to acquire this reputation at the expense of a proper devotion to the play. An inadequate amount of rest and sleep spells nervous strain. It will take supreme control to survive those terrible evenings of rehearsal when nothing will go right, and the cast is abnormally sensitive to the demeanor of the director. If he is calm and controlled, their own nerves will be soothed; if he allows himself to be ruffled and irritable he may expect the same behavior from the players. Temper out of control leads to temperament, which is not very highly esteemed today by serious theatre people.

Above all the director should possess a sense of humor, which is the same thing as a sense of proportion, and should exercise it to the full. He can do so only if he will refrain from draining away his nervous resources and exhausting his emotions by dramatizing every minor setback and magnifying it to the size of a near-catastrophe. A last word to the director who works under strain would be: "Remember that no one else will make the same allowances for your provocation as you do for yourself. Keep your sense of humor, your sense of proportion, and it will keep you."

CHAPTER THREE

Window Dressing

ᴀꜱꜱᴜᴍɪɴɢ ᴛʜᴀᴛ ᴛʜᴇ ᴅɪʀᴇᴄᴛᴏʀ ᴅᴏᴇꜱ ɴᴏᴛ ᴘʀᴏᴘᴏꜱᴇ ᴛᴏ ᴏʀɢᴀɴɪᴢᴇ a new group but plans to place his services at the disposal of a well-established community theatre, there are a dozen or more ways in which he may make known his availability. The *doyen* of all American drama monthlies, *Theatre Arts,* has a large circulation and tremendous prestige, and an advertisement in its columns during the spring and summer months should not fail to bring forth a number of replies. Other periodicals such as *Dramatics Magazine* and the *Journal of the Speech Association of America* have a wide distribution.

The National Theatre Conference maintains an efficient and comprehensive placement service and will gladly place on file, without charge, the name and qualifications of applicants for college and community theatre posts. The NTC Placement Service is regularly consulted by schools and theatres reporting vacancies, and while the Conference refrains from either recommending or disparaging any of the professionals on its books, it keeps such complete records of their work in previous posts that a prospective employer should have no difficulty in assessing the capabilities of any applicant.

In addition, all colleges with drama or speech departments keep files on their graduates, and frequently on other people who are known to members of the faculty, although when the time comes to make a recommendation any school will be excusably biased in favor of men and women they have trained themselves. A graduate of Carnegie should not expect to find himself high on the list of availables at Yale, and vice versa.

Above all, as in every profession, it pays to have a wide acquaintance and to maintain the proper contacts. Any director who plans to resign from a congenial post will usually let some of his friends know of his intention and give them the opportunity to apply if the friends have kept in touch with him, reported their addresses, and have hinted that they would be interested in such a job whenever vacant.

Besides keeping in regular touch with all his colleagues who are in seemingly snug jobs, an applicant-director should make it a point of honor to keep all the placement services informed about his movements and status. It is rather unethical, and poor business, too, for a man to put the word around in a dozen or more quarters that he is available and then, when he has discovered and accepted the most desirable offer, to keep his new appointment a dead secret from the very friends whose agency secured it for him. Cases are far too frequent where a college has kept active for several years the name of a desirable candidate, constantly submitting it to inquirers, while all the time the graduate in question has been happily employed in a job he had never reported to his school. The temper of community theatre selection committees is not improved by having to waste valuable weeks waiting to hear from well-recommended men who are no longer available. Sometimes the invitation will be eventually acknowledged with a lofty sort of disdain—the recipient not failing to mention that the committee's letter was delayed "owing to its having been sent to my old address," the implication being clearly that either the placement service or the theatre group should have made it their business to keep informed of the movements of celebrities. At other times the letter will arrive on time, but the recipient will be too busy, or too important, to send an answer.

After one or two such happenings any community group will

be inclined to decry all placement services as unreliable and make their choice from the men, perhaps less qualified, who make application out of a blue sky, rather than waste time sifting through a list of highly recommended candidates who may either write that they are unavailable or, worse still, not write at all.

The responsibility for keeping records up to date is squarely up to the individual. He has everything to gain by being quickly within reach when the ideal job comes up, and he alone stands to lose by neglect of his obligation to report his position.

After discovering a vacancy the applicant will open the skirmishes by a brief application indicating his availability and enclosing his favorite photograph. He may wish to mention his academic qualifications and where he is at present employed. It is not a good idea to fire all his artillery at one salvo; testimonials and press material (if he is sentimental enough to have preserved it) might well be reserved for a later exchange of shots. A good brisk correspondence, once it has been established that the parties to the prospective contract are intrigued by each other, is inevitable and desirable, but a personal interview should be sought without delay. Questions of policy and procedure are very difficult to discuss by correspondence. They should not even be touched on until after the director and his prospective employers have met face to face.

To enter into a contract for personal services of any kind without a give-and-take discussion of the obligations involved is a very risky proceeding. Courtship by mail has never been recommended as the basis for the ideal marriage, and harmonious relations in a community theatre cannot be guaranteed if the contracting parties have never met to exchange views. An interview is the only satisfactory culmination of the opening skirmishes effected by wire or mail, by telephone or by exchange of photographs. It is analogous to the ceremony of "meeting the folks" in that each side is on its best behavior, anxious to please, and ready to overlook small faults in the general betrothal atmosphere of good will and hopefulness.

Any member of the local group who dared to voice a doubt as
to the applicant's suitability would be suppressed as vigorously
as would the grouchy relative who objected to his prospective
nephew's table manners. He would be told he was too hard to
please, just as Uncle would be informed that times had changed
and perhaps reminded with some tartness that good men do
not grow on bushes. Any board of trustees which finds itself
in the happy position of having a plethora of applications from
well-qualified men can feel assured that they are offering an
adequate salary and, more important in a way, that their group
has a good standing in the professional circles where such
things are known.

Some few theatre groups who know in good time that they
will have a vacancy may send emissaries to the city where the
favored applicant holds a position, with the idea of seeing one
of his productions. The delegation will meet him, discuss his
work and his personality with the people around the theatre,
and then report back. It is not always necessary for the director
to have made application as long as it is known he desires to
make a change. Whenever a director can be viewed in action
in this way, both he and his prospective trustees are on fairly
safe ground.

The more usual practice is for a vacancy to become known
and for applicants to submit their credentials by mail. With
an applicant whose record indicates his superior suitability a
correspondence is begun and some details are discussed. Eventually an invitation to visit the city and meet the governing
body is extended to one or two applicants. Each of these men
will have read carefully the correspondence from the negotiat-
ing committee. He will have decided that the salary offered is
sufficient for his needs, that the policy briefly outlined will afford him freedom of expression and that, in short, he wants
the job.

There remains the necessary precaution of assuring himself
that the people he will have to work with will be sufficiently
talented to help him do good work, ambitious for their group

and their community, and friendly enough to make life pleasant and to encourage a long stay in their midst.

From the trustees' point of view it is essential that they make no mistake in their man. They are looking for one who will bring to his job an agreeable personality, the ability to make volunteers work harmoniously together, and the highest possible ideals and qualities of leadership. Both parties to the contract are aiming high. Let us see what happens.

The director can find no fault with the initial gestures of hospitality. Alexander Dean earned the gratitude of all community directors when he recommended a warm welcome for the professional in a strange city and argued the increased efficiency which could be expected as a result of the theatre leader being accorded a dignified standing in the community. In the days when his book, *Little Theatre Organization and Management*, was written that advice was really needed. There were many prejudices to be overcome and considerable spadework was necessary to build up the civic esteem which most directors can undoubtedly command today.

Oliver Hinsdell, writing *Making the Little Theatre Pay*, also did no harm when he drew up his specimen budget in which the largest single item was a salary of five thousand dollars for the director. Even if few of us ever came within range of that figure at least the mere suggestion helped to raise the sights of many budget committees, particularly in the days when the offer of a few hundred dollars to a high school dramatics coach for conducting evening rehearsals was considered a reckless extravagance.

The trustees and their friends are hospitable but they are also human, and it is a most endearing trait of our fallible humanity that we are always anxious to put the best face on things. On the occasion of the director-apparent's visit all faces will be shining with good will. The grouches and the dissenters will be kept in the background and the minority report will be recorded only by vague implication. Whether at a formal reception, a heart-to-heart talk with the board or executive committee, a tour of the plant and the city with a couple of board members who have time to spare, or "with a little group for cocktails," the director may expect to find friendliness, charm, and a wealth of amusing chatter.

He will have difficulty in keeping his head. "This is wonderful, these people are splendid, they are selling themselves to *me!* I must have made a good impression with my letters and my record, and that note from old Godwin must have helped. Must write and thank him when I get settled . . ." And so on, ad infinitum.

Now these good people, his hosts, are not willfully deceptive. They really are charming, and as individuals, nice to know. In the case of some of them there is a desperate need to justify themselves for, after all, the director who has just resigned on the grounds of incompatibility may have told his side of the story and warned the applicant to keep his eyes open. But in the main it is no more than a genuine desire to offer a welcome and give assurance of a co-operative spirit, and as such it is difficult to resist.

It is especially difficult if the director's economy is not, shall we say, on a sound basis and he is ready to jump at the first offer without proper knowledge of what is required of him. A friend of mine was once in that unhappy condition and accepted a post after nothing more than an exchange of letters. He met his trustees for the first time after journeying halfway across the continent to assume the post.

He had been anxious for a change of climate; the trustees had had good reports of his work and both of the parties to the contract apparently shut their eyes and picked blindly. Of course, everything of importance had either been omitted or side-stepped in the correspondence and, as might be expected, differences developed almost immediately. The board of trustees was rather dictatorial and so was my friend. When the first misconceptions arose, instead of making allowances for the inadequacies of "courtship by mail," both parties accused each other of misrepresentation. While the director was at fault in not having a proper understanding of his duties, the board of trustees was equally ill advised to entrust their plant, the enthusiasm of their volunteer workers, and their civic reputation to a stranger whom they knew only by correspondence, and to one, moreover, as in this case, with very positive views on policy and procedure which did not at all accord with the established practice of that theatre.

The first visit by the applicant, or director-presumptive, should not lack congeniality, but in their desire to appear friendly and co-operative the theatre group need not make a love feast out of what ought to be an occasion for critical analysis. Generally the atmosphere is one of undiluted good humor and no one wants to dispel this by raising controversial issues. To both sides this may prove to be a dangerous form of courtesy.

It is much more practical to remember that the director, however "presumptive" he may be, has not yet been offered a contract, still less has he accepted one. Both parties are still free, although the applicant is entitled to feel that he is, by reason of being invited to visit, one of only two or three left in the running. It is a fortunate situation for him if there are still other candidates being considered, as this means that the others may raise the same issues and ask the same, or different questions. If they ask the same questions the trustees will realize the importance of these points; if they ask different ones the subjects of the questions may be referred to each applicant for his opinion, thereby enlarging the scope of the discussions. The trustees will be able to compare their findings and make a much more informed decision, so that the man who is finally chosen will have very definite assurance that his attitude on practically every conceivable subject has been thoroughly reviewed and approved.

From the standpoint of the trustees it is well to meet personally more than one applicant. Despite good letters, a good photograph, and flattering recommendations, an application in person is the only safe basis on which to make a selection.

Therefore let the interview be as businesslike an affair as possible. Let the director make the fullest possible inquiries. Let the trustees do the same. More frankness of this kind would prevent many disappointments later on. Too many applicants are fearful of creating the impression that they are overcautious; too many trustees are afraid that a promising-looking man will withdraw in the face of too many inquiries about his experiences in a former position. A board of trustees, charged with the duty of appointing a man who may carry their theatre to greater heights of prestige, or wreck it beyond repair by wrong methods, is entitled to ask questions that may sometimes be brutally frank.

It might be interesting if each member of a board of trustees about to interview an applicant would agree to be responsible for concentrating upon a specific question, on some particular angle of theatre policy. One would, for instance, undertake to probe for facts about the director's preference in plays and his relative success in producing various types of play. Another would try to discover how systematically he conducted his rehearsals, and someone else might discuss the vexed question of closed or open rehearsals. The man's general ambitions, his long-range view of his job, his attitude towards community service, his hobbies, his keenness for some kind of sport, all these should be the subject of earnest inquiry. Whether he is comfortable as a public speaker, whether he prefers to address men or women, or both, should be discovered. Would he be happy or the reverse as a member of a luncheon club, is a point frequently overlooked. All these questions should be asked as a matter of course, and as freely answered.

I believe that when an applicant became aware—as he soon would—that the questioner was limiting his conversation to a specific problem and earnestly desiring information instead of merely making agreeable conversation, his answers would be quite unequivocal. With the present practice (that is, within my experience) of cloaking this desire for information under a running fire of small talk, and having six or eight of the trustees

"Do you like Noel Coward?"

at one time or other during the day ask nothing more pene-
trating than "Do you like Noel Coward?" very little satisfaction accrues to either party.

Any director of complete integrity will do his best to state
his convictions without hedging, but when questions are fired
at him from all sides without any ordered plan, and frequently
are quite as incriminating as the notorious "Have you stopped
beating your wife?" it is not surprising that the collated results
of the investigation will show many discrepancies.

This confusion is made vivid to me by recollection of the
experience of a fellow director who last year accepted a new
post after a hectic twenty-four hours of interview hospitality.
He had tried to answer the hundreds of queries, keep his head,
and proclaim his principles without any hedging. He believed
he had done a good job, but was quite astounded to discover,
after assuming his new post, that over half of the people to
whom he had talked understood him to say he had no time
for Shakespeare, about twenty percent distinctly recalled him
saying he would do Shakespeare only every three years, and
the rest were perfectly clear in their remembrance that he
would like to open each season with an Avon classic. He resigned in midseason, because the subject of Shakespeare was
not the only one on which his views were not clearly understood. He never had a chance.

Even with the suggested technique of specialized questioning, some misconceptions will arise. It would be better for any
applicant to answer all verbal questions truthfully, with no
idea of placating one or other of the inquisitors, and then,
before accepting a contract, sit down and again put into writing
his views and beliefs in the light of the new and obviously
important points that have been raised. A director cannot be
all things to all men. He may compromise on method but not
on principle, and everyone should know just how he stands
before he starts to work.

In addition to the trustees there will be a number of other
ardent theatre workers to whom the applicant will be exposed

during the interview visit. From these unofficial examiners, too, will come questions, and if the applicant is more than usually personable or sympathetic these volatile persons will make their own interpretations of his expressed views. Also, they will volunteer a great deal of information for his benefit, which may turn out to be most unreliable. The director should remember that the trustees are the people in whom he should place credence and to whom his views should be made clear. If he establishes a proper understanding with the responsible governing body he may expect to have their support and cooperation.

I would not for the world propose the discontinuance of the program of gracious functions which are now established practice with most theatres. A cordial welcome, both for the interview and for the actual induction into office, is good for the self-respect of all concerned. If a director has left a post where relations have become strained he needs to bask in the warmth of a friendly greeting, and the local group will be heartened by the praise he is likely to bestow quite sincerely on their city, their plant, and their personalities.

But the principal object of the interview is an interchange of views and opinions, the asking of many questions and the categorical answers made to them. If the trustees are often at fault in spending too much time dwelling upon the beauties of their residential sections, the director is more often to blame for sitting back exuding charm and neglecting to mention his ideals and principles, his enthusiasms and his pet peeves. He, too, should be asking questions, dozens of them, and he should be insisting quite politely on being completely answered.

Conference is an end as well as a means. It is the meeting of minds. There must be no concealment, no evasion. The first meeting, before the contract is proposed, is the time to discover differences and discuss them fully. After all, they may not be irreconcilable and courage and frankness will increase mutual respect and pave the way for a compromise acceptable to both sides.

Very few theatres have a policy clearly stated and carried out. Most of them are incorporated, and their charter leads off with some such phrase as: "The object of this non-profit corporation shall be the encouragement of dramatic and allied arts and the production of such plays as shall contribute to the education and enjoyment of the public." Or: "The purposes of this association shall be the production of such plays as, in the opinion of the duly-elected board of trustees, shall meet with public approval and support."

After which, as the law demands, they proceed to record the qualifications for membership and for voting, the amount of the annual dues, and the responsibilities of the various committees. The law requires that a corporation shall state its aims and objectives as succinctly as possible, but few theatres go beyond that legal requirement of a vague statement of purpose. They rarely put on paper any statement which indicates the goal of their efforts or the policy by which they hope to achieve it.

The reason for this omission may be that they prefer to be free in their interpretation of their duty to the public, or possibly that they feel incapable of a statement with so positive a ring that it might lead to dissension within themselves. Vague generalities seem to be the established rule and these do permit a freedom of action, but the man who is to be called director and held responsible for the execution of the theatre's policy must have a clear mandate. Even if the policy, general or specific, may vary according to the views of each elected group—and some theatres add complications by changing officers every year—the people in power should know where they are heading and what path they propose to take. Moreover they should be prepared to go on record to that effect.

The prospective director would be wise to start asking questions—of members of the board of trustees—as he alights from the train, and he should keep his inquiries going through all the parties, luncheons, and receptions which his hosts have arranged. At the same time he himself will be under a barrage of questions and if his views are positive and frankly stated there should be no misapprehensions on either side. If the director has his wife with him, so much the better. They will be able to confirm each other's memory of the interchange of question and answer, and when night falls on the exhausted couple they can compare notes to great advantage.

If their exhaustion is not too complete they would be well advised to make a written record of the information they have gained and given in return, and in the cold light of the following dawn, or reasonably soon after, they will be able to find in their notes an unimpeachable record from which to make judgment. Do they still want the job, or should they suggest that someone else be considered?

The trustees also will be pooling their impressions and opinions, and they may feel sufficiently impressed to offer the applicant a contract before he leaves town. Usually they prefer to weigh his qualifications against those of others they have met, and act only after due deliberation. The same caution is advised for the director, and even if he is offered the contract on the spot, he would be within his rights and exercising good judgment if he asked for time to consider. Contracts are much better signed at home, after careful perusal and calm reflection, than under the influence of charm, bonhomie, and the party spirit.

CHAPTER FOUR

According to the Rules

THERE IS NO SUCH THING AS A STANDARD CONTRACT FOR THE engagement of community theatre directors. This is probably because every theatre group believes that its situation is unique, that its public taste differs completely from that of any other city in the country, and that, in short, it has evolved the ideal method of approach to its problems.

Unfortunately this is very near the truth, and an attempt to institute a standard method of production procedure would be disastrous. The director must remember that most community theatres, whatever their size, have probably enjoyed twenty or more years of existence and have therefore learned their lessons the hard way. They have discovered by trial and error the workable methods and discarded the unworkable ones, and they are reasonably entitled to expect that their new director will conform to their findings.

The nearest to an ideal form of contract was drawn up nearly ten years ago by Carl Glick and Albert McCleery and appears in their book, *Curtains Going Up*. Admittedly it is one written by two directors with the best interests of their professional colleagues in mind, but it affords ample protection to both parties to the agreement. It is recommended reading for both director and trustees, who should modify its clauses in the light of local conditions and remember that several years have passed since it was drawn up. Each of the contracting parties should by now have some modifications to suggest as a result of experience, but the Glick-McCleery specimen covers the major points on which an understanding is necessary.

In the foregoing chapter, I have laid some stress upon the need for a statement of the theatre's policy. No actual reference to this may appear in the contract beyond, perhaps, a clause to the effect that the director understands the aims and purposes of the organization, has familiarized himself with the bylaws detailing how these purposes are to be achieved, and agrees to conduct himself in accordance with the same. It may have a pompous sound, but it is a fair demand for the theatre to make of its director.

Whether or not included in the actual contract, there should be a clear and comprehensive statement of policy drawn up by the governing body and available to the director before he accepts the contract. He should be able wholeheartedly to subscribe to all its clauses and conditions, or by the exercise of his skill in conference obtain such modifications as he believes essential to a proper working agreement. Unless he arrives at this complete understanding, he should not sign a contract; if he feels he can only accept the contract with mental reservations, he must not sign.

The general requirements of the contract will vary according to the particular type of theatre. The nonprofessional theatres fall roughly under four headings which cannot be distinguished by the title which the group uses; the nomenclature of these bodies is quite arbitrary and gives no clue to their plan of operation. They will include: Community Theatre, Community Players, Little Theatre, Civic Players, Civic Playhouse, Playhouse, Civic Repertory, or even just The ⸺ Theatre. The charter itself may tell nothing and the trustees may not be able to tell with certainty into which distinctive category their group should be placed. Nevertheless, if the questioning recommended in the foregoing chapter has been thorough it will also have been revealing, and the director will have received certain signals which if properly interpreted should enable him to place the theatre policy with some accuracy.

First, and most common of all, is the "theatre for the community." Groups of this type will aim at interesting the greatest possible number of participants. They will want large casts whenever feasible, plays of pageant dimensions, and committees of unwieldy size. Their play programs will contain literally hundreds of names: production workers, ticket sellers and ticket takers, coffee pourers and those (all of them) from whom the rubber plant used in Act II and the bric-a-brac in Act III were borrowed. They will demand plenty of new faces in each of the casts and that no player be used more than once a season so as to give others a chance to participate. They may have a casting committee to choose the players, a play selection committee to decide on the plays, and even if the productions do fall short of a high standard everyone around the theatre will have had a good time. The accent will be on self-expression, on offering the opportunity for participation to the widest possible circle of the citizenry. This type of theatre flourishes most satisfactorily in the cities of from 25 to 100 thousand population.

The second group might be called "the theatre for the drama," or the semiprofessional type. This flowers to best advantage in cities above the 100 thousand mark. It usually has the responsibility of augmenting the downtown theatre program which provides some few good road shows, and therefore can select its repertory from other than current Broadway pieces. It can even do Shakespeare or Shaw on occasion.

This second type of playhouse has a professional flavor in that the real work on production is often done by a staff of serious volunteers who are only faintly intrigued by the sight of their names in the program or the newspapers. On the part of both actors and backstage workers there is a genuine devotion to their avocation. The group will possibly contain some nonprofessional players of distinction, and if their time permits them to do so, they will play as often as the director's views on casting require their services. The principal consideration of such a theatre group will be a high standard of production and the consequent satisfaction of the audience.

In the rural areas, or in communities smaller than those served by these two types of theatre, the policy of "wide participation" is the rule. Again the accent is on numbers taking part, but as players and workers may not be so numerous as in the larger groups, a good and willing actor may appear in every play and the same faithful curtain-puller may haul on the rope every night of the season. The audience will receive some consideration, but as the community is a small one there will be a fine large-minded attitude of live-and-let-live. No brickbats will be thrown, the attitude of the audience being one of gratitude for a show of any kind, and the players will enjoy the satisfaction of performing to hearty, good-neighborly applause. There will be few jealousies, little backbiting and no cliques. Groups of this kind are likely to make up in congeniality and community spirit what they may lack in art.

The fourth species is the "pseudo-metropolitan." Around this theatre no one will want to do very much work, even in return for publicity, but everybody will expect it to be done somehow. The budget may provide the director with a small paid staff consisting of a technician-designer, a secretary, and a wardrobe mistress, as well as a janitor who may be coached to double as extra carpenter. The director may be able to organize his productions pretty much as he chooses as long as the results are good. The audience will be much more exacting than in any of the other types, being drawn from a population of a quarter-million or more. They want their theatre not only "as good as Broadway" but better, and they proclaim their sophistication by demanding bricks without straw and then complaining about the color of the product. To admit they were amused, thrilled, delighted, or even faintly entertained would be to deny their metropolitan outlook. They knock, and they knock, but they do keep on coming; perhaps just in order to have something to knock. And the director, if he can keep his equanimity, continues to produce the plays of his own choice to the best of his ability. In cases like this the director is the chief one to enjoy self-expression, and provided the audiences continue to come, even to scoff, he can keep on for a long time. His actors, however, might prefer a little more applause.

I have sketched these four types in deliberately broad strokes. Naturally they are not always as clearly defined as in these examples and the prospective director may have to peer very closely to detect microscopic variations. It is important that he be satisfied as to the general type of his new theatre, because he cannot—his training and his experience being what they are—carry out his obligations faithfully unless he is sympathetic to the expressed policy and the established practice of the group. For the trustees it is vital that they engage a man who has either worked before under similar conditions or one who, after having directed a group with a different policy, now desires, truly and honestly, to work under a change of conditions.

Something of these general aims should be stated, if not in the bylaws, at least in a few crystal-clear sentences in the letter or more formal contract which he is asked to sign. If after starting work his operations seem to be at variance with these instructions, he should be invited to a closed session of the Board and his actions there called into question. A frank discussion of the departure from policy should quickly clear the air. If it does not, then both parties would know where they stand and an amicable parting of the ways could be planned for the end of the season.

There is nothing very revolutionary about this suggestion, but in spite of its simplicity it is seldom utilized. Far more frequently a "situation" is allowed to develop, with the director nursing a grievance and perhaps farming it out among his intimates for further nourishment, and the individual members of the board gleaning gossip from anyone who will talk. The result of all this hole-and-corner work is that the case has been decided, sentence passed, and a breach created that no amount of later diplomacy will heal.

It is impossible to foresee every eventuality, and when a contract is discussed neither party wishes to pollute the friendly atmosphere by the suggestion that any trouble may possibly arise. (Incidentally, the same refusal to be realistic is the cause of so many married people dying intestate.) It is difficult but definitely necessary to take preventive measures against possible trouble by frank question and answer, and then to embody in the contract some clause which will make the settlement of differences easy, painless, and honorable to both sides.

All directors, and all trustees, too, should read the Glick-McCleery contract. As the authors themselves say of it: "This is a good contract. If you are a director, just graduated from Drama School, and get a contract like this—sign it!"

In spite of the implied bias in favor of the director, there is nothing in the document which takes advantage of the trustees. There are, however, some debatable clauses from the latter's point of view. These concern the powers of the director with regard to the selection of plays and casts. These problems have been the rocks on which many director-trustee relationships have split.

The practice regarding play selection roughly follows the pattern of the four types of theatre mentioned earlier in this chapter. The metropolitan type of theatre will most probably give the director a free hand. The second group, the "theatre for the drama," will possibly have a play-reading committee which acts in concert with the director. The groups which base their policy upon wide participation, both the urban and the rural types, will certainly have a play-selection committee, and in some cases the director is not even a member. This is an obviously unsatisfactory arrangement from the director's point of view and if the plays are selected by committee vote he should at least have a voice in the decisions.

Some few directors in each of these types of theatre are known to have a completely free hand in the choice of plays. This may not be so advantageous as it would appear, for the

The lone scapegoat

director may receive very little credit for a wise choice but he may take a frightful beating for an unfortunate selection. If it is his first season, in particular, he will be wise to enlist and welcome the advice of the local committee about the limitations of audience taste and acting material. There is no particular virtue in being the lone scapegoat.

On the subject of casting, the contract should specify that the director, and the director alone, is to select the players for the parts. However much he may prefer to rely upon local help in choosing the play, the professional is the only person equipped by training and experience to select the players. Any arrangement which takes from him this privilege and responsibility is calculated to reduce his efficiency and lower his standards. The contract should make it clear that he has a free hand in this matter, however much he may be restricted in others.

We will assume that the salary is going to be adequate, and properly guaranteed. Most groups are anxious that their director live in a good section of the city and be able to entertain on occasion, and most of them will give help in the search for the right place. Although the contract can hardly be expected to include a guarantee of desirable housing, some assurance that the director will have assistance in finding the right place might well be requested.

The manner in which the compensation is to be paid might be worth discussing fully. Most theatres will offer a fixed sum, payable monthly or even semimonthly, over a space of nine months. Some are willing to add the promise of a bonus or a percentage in order to secure the services of an exceptionally able man or to reward a director of several years service.

There are two principal ways to calculate the earning of the percentage; it may be either on the net operating profit (i.e., all income less all expenses) or it may be on the gross income only. There are some disadvantages to both plans. If the director is working on the net arrangement he may be tempted to cut down his production expenses and otherwise overdo the virtue of thrift so as to increase his share. If he works on the gross plan he may be overzealous for the box office and squander production money because none of those expenditures come out of his pocket. He may be virtuous and do neither of these things, but still be suspected of doing so. If any detractor therefore wishes to make capital out of such suspicions a lot of harm may result.

The safest way to forestall carping criticism on any salary arrangement is to have a proper understanding, written into the contract, about the operating budget. All expenditures connected with production should be under the sole control of the director. He should propose a budget for the acceptance of the Finance Committee, and once it is approved he should so plan his expenditures as to come out *just* on the right side. To be too economical is no virtue. It may impair the quality of the productions and is almost certain to result in a reduction of the amount budgeted for the following season. And to exceed the budget is to lessen the respect of the board for the director's abilities as a manager.

It is a mistake to economize on necessities such as paint, hardware, and small tools so as to purchase more expensive items of permanent equipment. My own experience has been that when the opportunity occurs to buy some extra lighting, some bargain in furniture, or some useful costumes it is better to place the request for the necessary funds squarely before the board and ask for authority to make the purchase. Such items, which are not expendables like paint, muslin, and nails, are legitimate capital expenditures and will be regarded as such by the business men on the board.

Expenditures other than on actual production, such as membership campaign expenses, additional furnishings for the front of the house, box-office salaries, landscaping of the grounds, and so on, cannot very well be controlled by the director, but there should be a clause in the agreement limiting the amounts which may be spent on such items. An actual experience may serve to illustrate this point.

One of my colleagues had completed his first season on

what he regarded as a very inadequate salary. The trustees refused to increase his guarantee for the second year, but proposed an arrangement which they felt would properly reflect
the results of his work. It was a very fair contract, calling for
him to share in the increase of membership over the figures for
his first season. Further, he was to participate in the net result
of operations on quite a generous scale. His budget was ample
and he felt confident of being able to mount the productions
quite richly and still come out on the right side.

After half the season was over both the membership and the
box-office income showed a large increase, with the budget so
far not half expended. The director began to see visions of a
large bonus almost the size of the original guarantee. But he
reckoned without the newly appointed president, who was
anxious to make a good showing for the theatre and made no
secret of his intention of "running the theatre at a profit." This
individual suddenly discovered that there were a number of
building alterations which must be attended to without delay; also that the very large dinner usually given to the membership workers at the end of the fall campaign would be more
fittingly staged before the current season ended. All these quite
considerable expenditures would of course be paid out of this
season's income and charged to the production budget. The
president was on the point of railroading the proposal when
the treasurer quietly reminded the board that they had a contract with their director which would be vitally affected by this
orgy of spending. It took no more than a minute for the building alterations to be forgotten and a motion to adjourn was
carried unanimously. Everyone, with the possible exception of
the president, felt a little embarrassed at having come so near
to an act of injustice.

Several members of the board of trustees went out of their
way to tell my friend what had happened and to offer a form of
apology for having overlooked the possible outcome of their
forgetfulness. The treasurer was watchful and conscientious
about his job and he knew, also, that the president had no

particular love for the director and would not go out of his way to protect the latter's interest in the contract. The director himself had not been present at the meeting. His agreement did not specifically call for attendance at board meetings and this one was held without his knowledge that anything but routine matters were to be discussed.

The director of any community enterprise should be required to attend all meetings of the trustees because he can immediately supply any desired information and at the same time protect his own interests, whether in working conditions or financial arrangements, by applying his expert knowledge to proposals he can show to be impractical. He has his finger on every detail of the workings of the enterprise, can report on progress up to the last minute, and is in a position to propose practical solutions to any questions that arise. On the other hand, each member of the board of trustees may have a dozen or more other organizational meetings to attend each month and, with all due respect to their powers of recollection, they cannot be expected to carry details in their heads without some prompting. In the case of my friend's experience with his bonus arrangement, a wary treasurer supplied the reminder, otherwise the other members of the board might have completely overlooked the matter of the contract.

The trustees should reserve the right to hold one meeting towards the end of the season at which, in the director's absence, his achievements are reviewed and the question of his re-engagement discussed, but at all other meetings their best interests require the presence of the man who has been entrusted with the destinies of the organization and who should alone be able to report frankly and completely upon every phase of the theatre's activities. Any board which makes a practice of meeting behind closed doors and relies upon secondhand information for a report on the principal business of the theatre is working in the dark; moreover, it is failing in its responsibility to the membership. Even if the principal item of every agenda may be an inquiry into the misconduct and inefficiency of the director, this is better than the secret conclave and the rumor session.

In the final analysis, no contract is worth more than the good faith of the men who make it. It is no more than a transcript of a verbal agreement, put on paper to refresh the memory rather than to embarrass the signatories by a legal quibble. The trustees are entitled to know how the director prefers to work because in that way he will be most efficient; the director has to know exactly what is expected of him. The compromise, arrived at with honor on both sides, is the contract. Whether it takes the form of a brief letter or a complicated whereas-and-whereunto, it serves to record the satisfaction with which both parties agree to enter upon their new relationship.

CHAPTER FIVE

Decently and in Order

EVERY BUSINESS CONCERN OF ANY IMPORTANCE MAKES USE OF A chart which defines the duties and interrelationships of its employees. This diagram is intended to show the delegation of authority from the shareholders through the board of directors down to the youngest office boy. It is the operating plan, referred to constantly, susceptible to some modifications from time to time, but always prominently displayed, clearly comprehended, and followed religiously by all those whose duties it illustrates.

Many community theatres make use of a plan of this kind; many more should do so and thereby avoid the frequent conflicts of authority and overlapping of duties which are bound to arise from a blind trust in the value of improvisation. The objection frequently heard is that a blueprint which lays down rules and regulations is a particularly nauseous form of regimentation; the volunteers declare they have enough of that type of dictatorship in their offices, their factories, and their stores. They share the universal hatred of regimentation, they dislike being pushed around, they come to the theatre in the evenings to escape from directives and surveillance of all kinds.

If they really feel as anarchistic as that, they should try to discover some more individual type of avocation, for the theatre is nothing if not a highly organized piece of mechanism which

A free-for-all of improvisation

depends for its smooth running upon discipline of the most rigid type. The theatre is one of the few workable autocracies left in modern society. A symphony orchestra is perhaps the supreme example, with the conductor's baton the most potent of all scepters. While no theatre director would covet the absolute powers of a Stokowski or a Toscanini, he does have to accept responsibility for the integration of the various elements and instruments of his production and must be prepared to accept the blame for any failure of the concerted effort.

A symphony cannot be played by a hundred musicians with as many varying ideas of tempo, and possibly even of volume and pitch, and a play cannot be produced as a round-table adventure, an opportunity for undisciplined self-expression or as a free-for-all of improvisation.

Harley Granville-Barker in *The Use of the Drama*, says: "A single voice, quieting all others—a single governing idea—the director speaks for the author"—for the author, not for himself; for the play, not for the production.

Barker was a rigid and imperturbable disciplinarian in the theatre, encased, as Nigel Playfair has put it, "in steel plated armor against impertinence," but he never regarded himself as a creator, merely as an interpreter. In the same spirit does Toscanini approach the performance of a Beethoven symphony, reverently, not with the idea of steeping his rendition in a personal and individual coloring, but merely enriching the beauty of the original hues. The interpreter as well as the creator is entitled to the rank of artist. What sometimes appears as despotism is no more than a proper appreciation of his own powers and evidence of his single-minded devotion to the writer or composer from whom he draws inspiration. His insistence that his shall be the "single voice, quieting all others" is not a pronouncement of omniscience, but the credo of a self-respecting craftsman with no false modesty regarding his ability to produce a properly unified interpretation of the work of the creative artist.

In pronounced contrast to this type of well-qualified interpreter is the virtuoso director. Great as was his ability to organize spectacle and train actors, the late Max Reinhardt was a virtuoso who saw himself as the creative artist and did not hesitate to brush the author to one side if the original meaning of the play stood in the way of some flamboyant piece of stage magic that could be effectively employed. In the wake of Reinhardt came his imitators, despots without his artistry, tyrants without his genius, all of them regarding the script as a peg on which to hang their Joseph's coat of theatrical tricks. To such virtuosi the meaning of the play is secondary to the importance of their personal legerdemain. Their names are programmed in larger type than the actor's; they take the cash, and the credit too.

This genus of theatre magician does not thrive in the community enterprises; there are other fields in which his talents find wider expression. The community leader prefers to regard himself as the faithful interpreter instead of the creative genius, and in the light of my knowledge of the prominent men in this field I can safely assert that they conceive of themselves as just that, and no more. In many cases their rather self-effacing approach to the script is misinterpreted and they are charged with a lack of creative ability because of their honesty and anxiety to deal justly with the author.

Whatever his approach, whether as the author's mouthpiece or as a partner with a controlling interest in the enterprise, the director will demand a free hand in the carrying out of his conception. He may defer to the author, but he cannot defer to a host of well-meaning coadjutors brimming over with helpful suggestions and with conflicting ideas for carrying them out. In any plan of organization the director must occupy the chair, must sit at the nerve center controlling the system of intercommunication between the co-operating elements, must delegate authority and assume responsibility, must set the pace and guide the course. He is the captain of the ship.

Instead of viewing him as some kind of despot (benevolent or otherwise) the timorous trustees who are confronted with a director's request for adequate control of authority would be wise to regard him as shipowners are compelled to regard the captains whom they entrust with the care and safety of their vessels. The owners cannot voyage themselves with every cargo; they select their skipper, vest him with authority and then remain on shore, warm, dry, and reasonably confident of the outcome. The analogy cannot be carried too far, because while it is not practical for steamship trustees to undertake long voyages it is the simplest thing in the world for trustees of dry-land enterprises to run around the corner to see what is going on, to ask awkward questions and to offer helpful suggestions, and to have anxieties, qualms, and scruples about the conduct of affairs as they see them. These fearful souls who see in a theatre director's demand for the necessary authority an attempt at self-aggrandizement and a denial of democratic principles would do well to ponder the words of Stark Young in *Theatre Practice*:

"In our American theatre the director is the man with the script in his hand who stands behind the whole performance of the play, who, in varying degrees, prescribes what the interpretation shall be, what the actors shall do, and trains them how to do it. He is the maestro, the coach, the general behind the rehearsals.

"The director is the artist who takes the drama as it is put into his hands and labors to re-create it in his own technical terms. And the drama, when it is re-created into those terms, becomes theatre and something that is different from what it was before. Directing is an art, or it is nothing."

This is not the apologia of an autocrat, but a cautious estimate of the dramatic interpreter's position by a man who is regarded as the most scholarly theatre critic in America.

Everything in the above passage points to the director as the final arbiter of the destinies of the produced play. The author has created, the director will re-create. Each production is a complete entity, and in order to produce a homogeneous result the element of autocratic authority must be introduced. The director must possess an organization properly developed to insure the swift and harmonious carrying out of his interpretation.

In a Broadway production the director has a more limited responsibility than in a community theatre. The professionals in charge of the various departments—the designers of setting, lighting, and costumes—are as expert in their own fields as the director in his. It is the producer (whether or not he has invested his own money) who co-ordinates the efforts and makes the final decisions.

In the community theatre the director is also the producer and must therefore supervise, control, and instruct all the elements of production. He may have the services of some salaried helpers, as in the case of the metropolitan-type theatres, but in the main his staff will be volunteer and his plan will be subject to unavoidable and sometimes unaccountable breakdowns and delays.

For this reason it is important that no department should be dependent upon the efforts of a single individual; there must be delegation of authority and sharing of responsibility.

The community theatre director derives his authority from the board of trustees who confer upon him the powers and responsibility for production in conformity with a schedule. While the trustees are the real producing authority, they remember that they are only theatre people by avocation with limited time to devote to this occupation and even more limited capacity for theatre details and technique.

Some individual members of the board, as chairmen or members of various committees, may figure as units in the production scheme, in which case they should cease to be trustees and must consider themselves as important only to the particular part of the work which concerns them individually. This exercise in split-personality is frequently attended by some difficulty.

The ideal arrangement would be for the trustees to exist only as a corporate entity, Olympian and remote, with none of its members participating in production details, but in practice this would deprive the director-producer of some of the most efficient workers. Many trustees earn their elevation to board rank by faithful service in one or other of the less spectacular jobs around the theatre and therefore place a high value upon their continuing usefulness. It is when they cannot separate the trustees from the staff workers that their schizophrenia causes anguish. They try to make the best of both worlds with frequently disruptive results.

A practical plan will undoubtedly fall short of the ideal, but one essential fact should be emphasized. Whether the departmental chiefs are dubbed "chairman of committee on so-and-so" or "head such-and-such" they should surround themselves with people sufficiently skilled to carry on that branch of production work for which the chairman (or "head") is held responsible. Any head carpenter or wardrobe mistress who takes the view that he or she cannot entrust certain work to any helper, can do it so much better and more quickly himself, etc., etc., should be replaced at the first favorable opportunity. This stubborn self-reliance may wreck a carefully planned timetable.

The director must organize every step which advances the preparation of the play. We are taking for granted that he is sufficiently equipped by training and experience to be able to plan a timetable. If he has a competent professional technical director, most of the work apart from the conduct of rehearsals will be shouldered by that functionary. If not, the director must exercise supervision over settings, furnishings and properties, lighting, wardrobe, make-up, and perhaps even publicity and promotion.

He will not be expected to do these things, merely to see that they are done. He must not set a bad example when the object of an organizational plan is that there must always be at least two people who know what particular job is next to be done, and how to do it. The director must try, hard as it sometimes may be, to stand on the sidelines and reserve his energies for the emergency, whenever that may arise. Opinions may

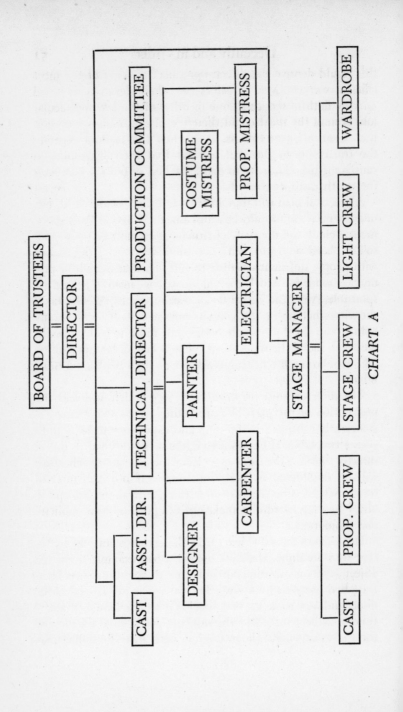

CHART A

differ as to when an operation ceases to be a difficulty and arrives at emergency status, but that is by the way.

Each department head should be sure that several other members of his working group not only know their own particular job but have an idea of the whole picture. If sickness, disaster, or merely pressure of business or domestic duties prevent the head from carrying out an assignment on schedule, there should be another staff member equally well informed who can step in to keep the work moving forward on schedule.

This will all sound absurdly simple and elementary to good organizers. It will appear as Efficiency Methods carried to excess to those who proceed by inspiration or the signs of the Zodiac, but the best kind of theatre has long outgrown the superstition that "a bad dress rehearsal means a good opening." That never was anything but a cowardly rationalization and a cloak for incompetency. Proper organization, with ample allowance for breakdowns, will permit not only one good dress rehearsal, but two, and even precede those two by a "technical" at which everything is present and in working order but perhaps not properly timed.

I am extremely diffident about offering a chart to express an organized production scheme because I have used many different blueprints at one time or another, dependent upon local conditions and upon the type of play being produced. These two are therefore the merest suggestions, to be adapted to individual requirements. As schools too frequently err in making their students' courses conform to a schedule when the schedule should be tailored to the students' needs, so the director should give much thought to actual conditions before putting on paper an operating plan intended to work. It may only succeed in setting up irritations and exaggerating difficulties. This must be an autocracy with the consent of the governed.

The succession of authority to the Stage Manager is a recognition of the established rule that after the final dress rehearsal this official becomes responsible for the smooth running of the show. As Alexander Wykoff says: "When the curtain is up,

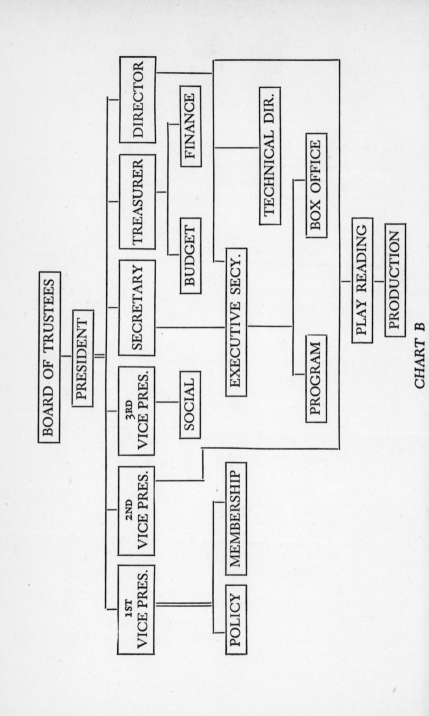

CHART B

the stage manager's responsibility is solely to the audience." By that time the director's work is finished and he can devote his efforts to creating a new organization for the next production.

Chart B attempts to express more clearly the relationship of the director to his trustees and the inter-relationship of the various other theatre officials. This distribution of duties has been utilized, with minor adjustments, in many theatres.

Some prefer to leave the first vice-president free to act merely as an alternate for the president, without charging him with responsibility for any particular committee. The placing of the second vice-president at the head of the so-called production committee is standard practice. So too, is the custom of bringing in the director as co-chairman of this body which, as I shall try to explain in the following chapter, is an advisory rather than an operational one.

Naturally the treasurer will head those committees which concern finance (the raising of money) and budget (the spending of it) and some groups may prefer to leave the secretary as merely a recording officer and not burden him or her with the business of committees. The important thing is that the director shall supervise the production activities. The trustees are left in undisputed control of all the functions of the theatre except those which they must delegate to their professional employee if he is to function to his highest capacity.

CHAPTER SIX

Pride and Prejudice

‹‹

INSEPARABLE FROM THE OPERATION OF HUMAN RELATIONSHIPS IS the committee habit. It is a growing one, which in a sense is an awesome commentary on our increasing reluctance to accept individual responsibility; we prefer to share the burden of a decision with a group of our fellows rather than chart our own course of action and be prepared to sink or swim as a result.

A less jaundiced view is taken by those people who regard committee procedure as the supreme embodiment of the democratic principle, the bulwark against dictatorship, and the universal solution for all problems. At its best the committee method does represent an honest human attempt to resolve difficulties by negotiation instead of by decree. The worst that can be said of committees is that they are sometimes so unwieldy, because of size, that no clear-cut decisions are ever made, and that the habit of appointing committees to settle every question that arises can be overdone, to say the least. Some easygoing executives have a faith in the magic of this procedure that borders on the superstitious.

Committees fall, quite roughly, under three distinct headings: the first might be called The Committee To Report; the second, The Committee To Decide; and the third, The Committee To Do. Of these the first is the one chiefly beloved of Roberts, Gleason, and the other authorities on parliamentary procedure. It is also the one which is the stand-by for the good-natured executive type. For him the appointment of a "Committee To Report" is the way out of every difficulty, for by making this appointment he hopes to shelve the whole matter and avoid having to make a decision. It is usually a profound shock to him when he accidentally appoints a chairman who, with excess of zeal, actually calls a meeting, goes into the matter, and makes a report.

The capable executive, of course, makes his appointments only after proper consideration, and really expects results. Moreover, he usually gets them. At Shreveport, Louisiana, with Clyde R. Minor as president, no chairman appointed to unearth facts or to propose a practical solution to a problem ever failed to report on time. Mr. Minor is established in my memory as the ideal president. The board of trustees was always well informed and at the regular monthly meetings they handled most of the theatre business as a committee of the whole. They were able to do that principally because attendance, over the five seasons I was there, averaged almost ninety-five percent and the meetings took place in an atmosphere of great friendliness but were at the same time quite businesslike. When board meetings are as well attended as in this case, and all members keep themselves well posted, there is less need for the constant appointment of committees to report on this or that.

The Committee To Decide is explosive material for the inadequate president to handle. It takes a high degree of confidence and good judgment to make appointments and be willing to confirm the findings of a body appointed "with power to act." Within certain limitations, as, for instance, budgetary ones, the standing committees of the theatre operate under this heading. The groups charged with the maintenance of house and grounds, or library, and with conducting activities of a social nature (hospitality) such as dress-rehearsal suppers and cast parties all have a great measure of freedom in their operations and the chairmen of these groups will be selected only after a great deal of thought. These committees, appointed in the summer or early fall, hold office and do their jobs without further supervision until the end of the season the following May or June.

With most of these committees the newly appointed director will have little contact unless, as a matter of courtesy, he is informed of their plans or invited to attend one of their meetings. His attendance at board meetings will afford him the same information as to the workings of the standing committees as that possessed by the board of trustees.

The committees which appear in Chart B in the foregoing chapter, such as Finance, Membership and Box Office, are all standing committees. The director may frequently be invited to attend meetings of these bodies either as a matter of courtesy or because his opinion may be valuable. Unless his status is that of managing-director he will have only an academic interest in their problems.

The two permanent committees on which the director should always be invited to serve "ex-officio" are those concerned with Production and Budget. With the decisions made by these groups he is vitally concerned.

If we accept the general meaning of the word "committee" as describing a group of people who meet, deliberate, and either make decisions or recommendations, then the third type, The Committee To Do, is not a committee at all. The army would describe it as a "detail." Its job is to do things, with might and main, with hand and brain, with tooth and claw. These are no extravagant figures of speech when speaking of such bodies of ardent production workers as the committees on costume, properties, décor, and so on. These people do not congregate in a smoke-filled room and most of them are so constantly in violent motion that to refer to them as members of *standing* committees would be a contradiction in terms.

On the assumption of his new post a director may find that the members of the Production Committee have already been selected or reappointed from the previous season. This is almost inevitable since a good deal of preparation has to be accomplished during the summer and early fall. In any case the newly arrived director will have no knowledge of the temperaments or abilities of the volunteer workers and should therefore be grateful for machinery already set up and in operating order. As the season develops new and capable workers will be discovered, while some of the veterans may prove to be less efficient than they appeared at the beginning.

It is always a debatable point whether a director should make his own selections or accept the appointments of the president. Since all the books on theatre organization have been written by directors it is not surprising they all take for granted that the committees which work closely with them will be their own appointees.

This can be regarded as carrying autocracy and omniscience a step too far. While no director can hope to achieve the best results when any one of his committee heads lacks either a willingness to co-operate or sufficient ability for the work, the leader must exercise patience, remembering that he is also supposed to be a teacher. Nor can he afford to mistake willingness for experience, or even for adaptability, yet he must give the usually earnest volunteer the benefit of every doubt. Also he must approach each problem in personal relations as separate and individual, being prepared to believe that this particular head of a committee may have worked admirably with the previous director, whose successor's way of doing things, and even his vocabulary, may be so radically different that adjustment has to be made slowly.

If patience and long-suffering do not bring about more fruitful relations, the alternative to a rupture might be an appeal to the president to whom the director owes a primary loyalty and on whose tact and discretion he should be able to rely. The president will usually be able to suggest some change of tactics by which proper collaboration may be achieved. To lubricate the theatre machine is a duty which any good president will be willing to share with the director, and both of the men should feel absolute security in a frank discussion of organizational problems. Both of them will regard their interchange of views as top-secret business since it should be obvious that they are handling material which is almost atomic in its potentialities. A director who makes public complaint of some volunteer's inadequacy or a president who passes around the word that the director cannot get along with so-and-so are both lacking in fitness for their duties and are laying the foundations of a wider dissension.

Disregarding entirely the question of their ability, the members of any committee, and particularly its chairman, must be presumed to have a pride in their contribution. The esprit de corps of the theatre challenges their best efforts and even those workers with a sense of humor will resent being ridiculed or taken for granted. The director has to proceed on the assumption that all committees genuinely desire to give the greatest possible assistance and that their efforts deserve recognition and appreciation.

I recall an incident recounted to me by an active adherent of a theatre whose director had suffered a steady decline in prestige for three seasons. His introductory production, done with a small cast in one setting, was carefully produced and cordially received. The second production of the first season was to be on a grandiose scale with a large cast and period costumes. Volunteers were numerous and a costume committee was assembled in the rehearsal room where about a dozen ladies operated sewing machines every day in almost sweat-shop rhythm. This director had to pass through this room on the way to his office. My informant, herself one of the toilers, said that the foolish man (her own phrase was less temperate) passed through that hive of activity a dozen times a day without so much as a "hello." He seemed quite unconscious of the fact that these women were working to achieve an effect which would contribute to the ultimate success of one of his productions—one that was later hailed as a directorial masterpiece. To him went both praise and a good salary, while his good volunteer craftswomen were denied even a nod of greeting. It is small wonder that his stock went into a decline and it became more and more difficult for him to find workers for his committees.

I must confess that I myself have been guilty of failure to make the proper gesture of appreciation on several occasions. The professional is so apt to take for granted, and "in the line of duty" what the volunteer views as an exceptionally gallant achievement. Professional leaders have to remember always that nothing is routine when the rewards are not monetary, and that in the eyes of the contributor even the smallest donation of time and enthusiasm is exceptional and therefore worthy of recognition.

Above all, the chairmen of the committees deserve the director's confidence and courtesy at all times. These are the women who do the impossible around a theatre, who discover the most inaccessible "props" and unearth just the right pieces of furniture. They receive little reward beyond the thrill of the chase and a reasonable appreciation of their labors. I say reasonable, because at the other extreme from the director who treats his helpers as so many anonymous robots is the cheerleader who slaps so many backs that everyone eventually hides when he comes into sight. The wise community theatre leader will choose a middle path.

Apart from the board of trustees the most important group of people with whom the director must maintain satisfactory relations is the production committee. Many theatres do not appoint such a body. The director himself is expected to appoint a production staff. The larger or the more solidly established the theatre, the greater the chance that the staff procedure will be followed. This is logical, since in the course of time a number of volunteers become exceptionally skilled and capable of working without supervision. Also, if the director has been in office several seasons he will then be enjoying the confidence of the trustees to the point where his recommendations will be followed without question.

The committee method is used by the smaller groups and those whose policy accents wide participation. It is also the safeguard of those groups who shrink from granting their director too much authority or counting on his staying long with them. Many community theatres believe that directors should move every four years.

In cases where this policy is in force it is not surprising that trustees hesitate to allow a director to build an organization which will owe him a great measure of personal loyalty and will perhaps disintegrate on his departure. They prefer the continuity of the committee system, with many volunteers being fed into the hopper each year for training, and so being prepared for the heading of committees in coming seasons.

The production committee may well be headed by one of the vice-presidents, as indicated in the Chart of Organization, appointed (or elected) especially because of aptitude for that job. He or she will then be free to appoint the sub-chairmen on playreading, décor, properties, costumes, etc. These chairmen will form the actual committee to plan the work of production. The vice-president will conduct the meetings and be responsible for keeping the various sub-chairmen up to the mark on their assignments. The director will attend each meeting, outline the plan of work, and set the timetable.

The most successful operation of this plan in my experience involved no more than two meetings of the general committee for each play. Good planning by the particular vice-president insured that every member of the committee had read the play in advance of the first gathering, which took place about five weeks before the date set for each opening. The committee heard the director's outline of his conception, the style and décor proposed, his explanation of the difficult "props," and then asked questions which arose either from their reading of the play or from hearing the director's production plans. The committee then dispersed, to meet again in about a week, by which time each chairman had selected the particular workers she considered most suitable to handle the work on the play.

This required quite a little exercise in judgment and most of the committee heads went to some pains to appoint the people best fitted for each individual production. The property mistress, for example, who could handle a quick-moving farce-comedy or a mystery, with dozens of trick pieces like guns, telegrams and comic packages, might not be the one to set the stage for a comedy of manners, with afternoon tea à la Lonsdale, or be calm in the presence of the grandeurs of the banquet in "The Swan." And vice-versa.

In my experience with this arrangement these appointees became my production staff and were called together as soon as possible for a preliminary discussion of problems. The vice-president, as chairman of production, attended this meeting in the role of co-ordinator only. From then on these workers ran their own departments, working in consultation with me or the technician.

A plan similar to this one is offered as a fair compromise between the two rather conflicting ideologies of Committee and Staff. It preserves the theatre dynasty as against the director's creation of one of his own, and it insures continuity, because the breaking up of the work among a great number of people every year provides training not only in the actual production work but in executive operations. The director has a staff responsible to him, but its personnel changes to some extent for each production and the cry of "clique" cannot be raised with any justification.

In the final analysis the relationship between director and committee workers is determined by affection and mutual confidence. The leader must go out of his way to discover the approach by which harmony may be achieved. And the proper vocabulary is important to proper understanding. Even technical terminology differs in various parts of the country. In some parts the "stage braces" may be fixed to the floor by "stage screws," in other cities they are known as "stage pegs" or even "stage pins." And "teaser" and "tormentor" should, of course, mean the same thing, but people who are not twenty-four hours a day dealing with such mechanisms cannot quickly remember that in the theatre they are very different. It is better to point than to yell in desperation.

A general course in semantics might well be part of a community theatre director's training. I believe in the dangers of "unconscious assumptions about language." In the theatre people are expected to deal in words, in a wealth of expression not available to the everyday world. Even if the technical terms can be simplified to the point where everyone is clear as to what is meant by a "dimmer," the "apron," or the "flies," there are still pitfalls in general communication. And not only the words themselves but the actual tone of voice may be misinterpreted.

A personal experience might serve in illustration of this, as I recall an occasion when my choice, both of words and tone of voice was unfortunate and led to confusion, delay, and hurt feelings. At the technical rehearsal some small property or other was not in place. The action stopped while the property mistress hunted for it. Since I remembered having seen it in the wings just before rehearsal started I called out that it might be found "on the barrel, offstage left." Someone called out "thanks" and we waited, but nothing happened. I repeated the information, in my best clear voice—to a great silence. After a third try, my exasperation mounted and I came down the aisle, shouting out "on the barrel, the BARREL!"

The stage manager came on stage waving deprecatory hands and screening his eyes against the lights. "Where did you say you'd seen it?" By this time I was on stage, striding angrily in the direction of the barrel which was, of course, exactly where I had seen it, and on it was the missing "prop." Triumphantly I displayed it, to an awkward and embarrassed silence. Someone tittered nervously, which did not help, but I gave the word to go on with the play. Nothing else marred the progress of the rehearsal, but the atmosphere was rather tense, and I felt it was not one of our best evenings.

It was not until several weeks later that someone told me

the inside story, which was that no one had had the slightest idea of what I was saying. In the first place, after my first message from the back of the house my voice grew higher in pitch and more English in inflection and what the backstage people heard sounded to their Southern ears like "battle." "Now, if you had only said you'd seen it on that keg, Talbot, we'd have known where to look." We need semantics, indeed, and we need self-control, particularly when things don't go too well at rehearsals.

It must be admitted that the staff plan, with a nucleus of skilled workers always at his disposal, is the easiest for the director. To have to train new workers every month, while more capable ones wait on the side lines for their turn, is sometimes disheartening, but it is part of the job, especially if the theatre is one definitely pledged to what I have referred to as the policy of wide participation.

Under this "wide" system the first few productions may have to be a little less than artistically satisfying, because to reject one after another of the rather distressing pieces of bric-à-brac submitted by some willing worker would be to impugn the taste of the chairman who appointed her. It is in cases like these, which occur only too frequently, that semantics are invaluable. The exact use of language is of tremendous importance. So is facial composure. Any actual criticism of an individual volunteer should come from the chairman of his or her committee. That is the privilege of the chairman. It is not the director's. I made the mistake of so stepping out of line once, and it took many months to mend my fences.

Even if the director is called upon for a direct comment on a piece of work or a contributed property, there are many more ways of rejecting it than by the use of the word "appalling." Or, as one director of my acquaintance did, by flinging the offending chair down the aisle after the retreating figure of the woman who had just brought it in.

This particular extrovert was actually re-engaged for the following season after this exhibition, but that was many years ago, when directors were not supposed to be quite normal, and temperament was at a premium. Carl Glick used to say the community theatre needed a combination of God and David Belasco. Nowadays they expect, in addition, the career diplomat and the psychologist.

A cynic once observed that the ideal committee consisted of three members, two of whom were permanently out of town. But he was no realist. The committee habit is deeply ingrained in the American way of life, and the wise procedure for the most rugged individualist is to accept this fact and shape his course accordingly. He may not get things done as fast as he would wish, but he will gain a lot in the way of human companionship, a breadth of acquaintance and a great satisfaction, if he does not allow committees to get in his hair, but enjoys them as people, and learns to persuade rather than compel them to his point of view.

CHAPTER SEVEN

Shakespeare, Shaw, or Saroyan?

THE PLAY IS OVER. THE CURTAIN COMES DOWN AND THE APPLAUSE is generous. Now the actors are all out on the stage, taking their calls—one, two, three, perhaps four. As the applause takes on the eventual perfunctory note the curtain comes down once more—and stays down. The lights come up, and the ushers fling open the exit doors and stand aside as the audience streams out of the theatre.

Scraps of conversation overheard, greetings, and comments; a few voices louder than the rest, repeating some phrase from the play's dialogue—perhaps a laugh, some murmurs of satisfaction and pleasure. Then, with disturbing clarity, the inevitable sour note: "Oh yes, they were all very good, but I wonder who chose that play."

Well, who did? And why? Who *does* choose the plays for the community theatre? And how do they go about it?

Usually there exists a committee called either "Playreading" or "Play Selection." There is no significance, by the way, in the distinction implied by those titles. Many committees which go under the name of "Playreading" actually select the repertory, while quite frequently the ones supposedly dedicated to "selection" act only in an advisory capacity. The need for semantics again!

The name under which this committee functions, therefore, is no guide to the actual duties it performs. By whatever name, this is the most hard-working committee around the theatre. It is also, without question, the most potent. It is also the least appreciated. It gets all the kicks and none of the ha'pence. The director chafes under either its restrictions or its instructions, the audience writes it no fan letters and I have never known any actor shake its collective hand in gratitude for a meaty role. The committee goes on reading plays.

The custom of entrusting the selection of the theatre repertory to a group of interested members stems from the early days of the Little Theatre movement. Rehearsals were conducted, rather than the plays directed, by teachers of expression, high school drama coaches, and even exceptionally courageous members of the amateur groups themselves. It was quite logical that these volunteer directors should need and even welcome the advice of a small interested group of play-readers and others familiar with the taste of the local audience.

With the advent of the specialists (the full-time professionals) many of the little theatres were persuaded to relinquish the privilege and the bother of choosing plays to these appointed leaders. After all, these men were professionals, they presumably had hundreds of plays at their fingers' ends and they spoke with the voice of authority. The local committees were content to sit back and rest from their labors.

Unfortunately not all of these newcomers were good showmen; they took little account of local preferences and prejudices, although they had plenty of their own. If they came from Broadway, as many of them did, they frequently chose plays in which they had played a small part in New York, but taking care to play the lead when they staged them on Main Street. The local stars were justifiably resentful at having to play a succession of supporting roles. In other cases the Broadway actor-director saw no harm in love scenes or situations which aroused violent tremors in the provincial breast; or his devotion to plays with pungent dialogue was offensive to audiences to whom "durn it" was risqué and "damn" the utmost obscenity.

Other men came from the colleges, where the classics had been their staple diet. They either knew nothing of current American drama (except by classroom study) or they pretended to despise it, regarding themselves as men with a mission to minister to the heathen. Mencken and Nathan were busy burning up "Boobus Americanus" in those days and the wise (but so young) men from the East were anxious to light some fires of their own.

It would be charity to suggest that these early directors were born twenty years too soon. At any rate their taste in plays quite often lacked the fullest appreciation, and theatre trustees who had so blithely surrendered their right to a voice in play selection almost fell over themselves in their anxiety to write restrictive clauses into the contract they made with the next man.

There were, of course, prominent exceptions. Some of the new career men combined good taste with discretion and by making haste more slowly they earned the growing confidence of their trustees and their public. Such directors as these are still occupying the posts they assumed fifteen or twenty years ago, suffering no restrictions in their choice of plays and enjoying the support of a discriminating public. But in the great majority of community groups the final authority is still the committee.

There cannot be enough praise for the committee frankly dedicated to the reading of plays as an assistance to the director (who usually does not read as many new ones as he should), and advising him as to their possible reception by the audience. If this committee pools its opinions and comments, the director will be in possession of much valuable information, more especially if he is newly appointed. He will still reserve the right to argue the playing possibilities of some script that his advisors may have found tedious. He may know that some comedy whose dialogue sparkles from the printed page will prove monotonous and undramatic on the stage and he will be able to say so, knowing that his judgment, as that of a trained theatre professional, will be respected and followed.

Very few theatres are fortunate in possessing members who are avid readers of dramatic literature and are also good judges of play values. One I knew used to combine the office of chairman of the playreading committee with that of house manager, and thereby gained invaluable knowledge of audience reactions by hearing the lobby comments at every performance. His was a very real theatre wisdom which is all too rare. Far more frequently directors have cause to complain of arbitrary armchair judgments made by committees who never see any rehearsals and sometimes not even a performance of the plays they promote so vigorously.

The problem of responsibility for play selection may be solved in one of two ways. When the contract is being discussed, the director, if he is justified by training and experience in making the demand, should insist upon freedom of choice for his first season at least. He may profess himself anxious to have the advisory services of a committee, but he should be entitled to retain veto power.

If, on the other hand, he is only recently graduated and has a becoming modesty about his powers of judgment, he may well agree to share the responsibility with a committee for the first two or three seasons. At the end of that time he should be justified in requesting a freer hand and be prepared to stand or fall by his wisdom of choice. His judgment of plays is part of his professional equipment. To deny him the use of it is to reduce his efficiency. It is like sending a boxer into the ring with his right hand tied behind him and then blaming him for losing the fight.

That is the point which eludes so many governing bodies when, jealous of their prerogatives, they hesitate to delegate the selection of plays to their professional appointee. A director who stages a succession of unfortunate plays will hurt himself

far more than he will the group, for he need not look for a re-
newal of his contract even after his first season. If the trustees
are fearful that their audiences will be subjected to outhouse
humor or left-wing propaganda they probably have no one but
themselves to blame. The director's taste in such matters
should have been quite thoroughly reviewed in correspondence
and at the interview, and if any doubts remained a brake could
have been put on his subversive tendencies by an unequivocal
clause in the contract. There are all sorts of ways to prevent a
director from exploiting himself or his political views to the
detriment of the theatre which employs him.

Far more damage to harmonious relations is liable to occur
when a director is under contract pressure to produce plays
which strike no fire from him, which he regards as unworthy of
his efforts or those of the players, or which he knows he cannot
cast or stage to the proper advantage. It is not always easy to
convince the committees that these objections are valid, and
the proponents of some obviously unsuitable play often return
to the attack every season with amusing persistence. Even if
the stage of crisis is never reached and the bickering remains
good-natured, many a director has been known to throw up
his hands, swallow the bone of contention, and produce the
play against his better judgment. If the production is successful
—and it often is—the persistent advocates will feel their judgment amply vindicated and bring heavier pressure to bear in
future controversies. If the production fails, the director runs
a grave risk of being accused of "selling out" in order to justify
his original opinion, and thereby may incur enmities that will
pursue him up to the day of his departure.

No director can remain permanently insensitive to sniping,
but if he is willing to pick up and rehearse every script which is
handed to him he is no artist; he is not even an honest craftsman. A self-respecting plumber or carpenter will refuse to work
with shoddy equipment. Even a director who lacks the full
stature of an artist might at least be given credit for the desire
to work with good tools. The community director does not

have the wealth of Broadway at his command when he picks a cast; it is an added handicap when he is compelled to rehearse these players in a play which affords him no inspiration.

In case I may appear to have drawn too vivid a picture of the martyr-director and the tyrant-trustees let me say that it is not overdrawn according to complaints from colleagues of mine at a dozen or more theatres up and down the country. There is one group in the middle west which between 1933 and 1938 employed six directors. One year was sufficient for each of the first five. Also, the theatre had a gradually mounting deficit during these years. The sixth director analyzed the situation, called for a revision of policy, and was able to lead the group to solvency and harmony before the navy claimed his services in 1942.

A happier experience was my own at Shreveport, where the board used to function as a "committee of the whole" on play selection. At every meeting one member would plaintively inquire? "What about Dear Brutus?" Now there were many reasons why we were not ready to do that particular play and they were all carefully, and in the best of humor, recited to him every time. If he ever was absent, there was always some facetious fellow-member who would submit the familiar query. Dear Brutus was a permanent item on the agenda.

Finally, in my last season, our finances allowed us to consider paying the high royalty that a Barrie play always commands. Soon after the decision was made to pay this fee I discovered a young actress who could realize the part of Margaret. We did Dear Brutus, and everyone was happy, including myself. It had been as much against my principles to do an inferior production because the right players were not available as it was for the budget committee to authorize an excessive expenditure before income justified it.

Every theatre has to maintain a nice balance in its choice of plays between giving the public what they want and what they ought to want. A theatre has to pay its bills and it also has to do some plays that will justify its claim to be other than purely commercial. The day of the subsidized group is over. So is the era of the "art" theatre which performed intermittently before cheesecloth draperies to a shivering coterie in an unheated barn. Theatre is business now, but perhaps no less genuinely artistic than in the days of unbalanced budgets.

To attract the larger and more general audience of today the play selectors must appeal to wider interests. It is unfortunate that this conception of their duties often leads them to concentrate on recognized Broadway successes and to neglect the far greater library of dramatic literature outside Mr. Burns Mantle's lists.

I cannot go all the way with Sean O'Casey in his view that it is better for amateurs to do good plays badly than bad plays well, but an occasional attempt at an exceptionally fine play should be justified even if the production does not quite come off. A dull level of competence, with players consciously or unconsciously imitating the original Broadway cast, will prove monotonous for everyone. It will stunt the growth of the actors, lend no prestige to the repertory and eventually lead to a loss of interest by the principal supporters.

But an occasional stab at the seemingly impossible, the production of a play that no one has seen performed but which by its quality of writing and the truth of its characterizations gives promise of excitement, with scenic effects that have never been pictured in a magazine but which challenge the ingenuity of the production workers, with wealth of dramatic contrast that will inspire the director's best efforts—this type of bravery wins battles and it also wins supporters. Everyone around the theatre will work their hardest on something that is different, and difficult. Every theatre should tackle something too big for it at least once in a season, for the good of its soul. And the box office, paradoxically enough, will not suffer.

The question of casting is bound up inextricably with the selection of plays. Some directors may not agree with this point, and some community theatres flatter their director by the implication that he is sufficiently a genius to be able to cast a play from the most unpromising acting material. While appreciating the compliment the honest professional will admit that none of his productions can be any better than the actors who play in it, and while it may be true that certain run-of-the-mill comedies can be performed equally well by W, X, Y, and Z as by A, B, C, and D, the more difficult the play the greater is the need for people of exceptional suitability. The play-readers would do well to remember this while they are at work. My *Dear Brutus* fanatic at Shreveport was persistent, but he was not unreasonable. Not all others are as patient as he was, and some are apt to feel injured if their suggestions are not acted upon immediately. The director must give reasons for his inability to act immediately on every suggestion. The committee should be able to accept the reasons in good faith.

As a rule it is well to avoid "star" plays where the principal player carries the whole show. To observe this rule too rigidly, however, would be to deprive some good actors of the chance of playing such plays as *Counsellor-at-Law*, *The Second Man*, or *Cyrano de Bergerac*, and the popular leading ladies of fluttering their wings in *Candida*, *Hedda Gabler*, *Biography*, or even *Susan and God*. It is never desirable to choose plays as vehicles for particular players, but it is the policy of wisdom, if the director is to get the desired results, to consider the available talent when each play is selected.

We shall assume the existence of a committee and that its function is to discover and read plays for the director's consideration. Such a method was in operation at the Dallas Little Theatre during its entire existence, and the list of its productions is almost a classic of repertory. * The director is grateful for suggestions, is willing to accept advice, is gracious in making objections, and derives a great deal of moral support from the discussions and friendly meetings. But he himself, and he only, chooses the plays. That is one method, favored by

* See Appendix.

the larger theatres or those whose directors enjoy the confidence of their trustees because of long tenure.

An alternative plan which has many merits involves the actual selection of the plays by a committee of which the director is an active member. He may submit a list of plays, say fifteen or twenty, from which the program will be chosen, or the other members may submit to him a similar number from which he will choose the appropriate six, seven, or eight. This is a quite workable plan, used by many theatres. Agreement is usually reached on the pattern of the season's schedule before the lists are compiled. Of perhaps seven plays, are as many as four to be comedies of one sort or another? Do they want to do Shakespeare this year, or some other period classic? Does Saroyan meet with favor? Which of the Shaws—Bernard or Irwin—or both?

A properly diversified program is very important, and the director will be the best judge of the type of play to do at one or another time during the season since he alone knows the style in which he intends to direct the pieces. To illustrate this point, a play like *The Male Animal* will serve as example. To some directors this Thurber-Nugent work is just a noisy romp, while at least to one director of my acquaintance it is a play of much social significance, and his production laid great emphasis on the author's message about academic freedom and played down the farcical elements completely.

Viewed from his angle *The Male Animal* could very well appear in the schedule between two light pieces without impairing the variety of the pattern. In the same way S. N. Behrman's *Rain From Heaven* could, in the years when its message was more topical, be presented as a powerful preachment against Fascism, or (as I have seen it done) regarded as merely a piece of delicious high comedy. It is on such plays as these that the hand of the director is most clearly seen.

C. B. Purdom (*Producing Plays*) lays down four very simple rules for the choosing of a play. He asks himself will it please, first himself as director, secondly the players, then the audience, and lastly he asks whether its production is practicable. Under this last question he lumps together the questions of casting, staging, and costuming and perhaps also (though he does not mention it) the size of the royalty payable.

This is sound advice. It confirms my thesis that the director will do his best work on a play which has magnetism for him. It underlines the importance of having the players enthusiastic about their vehicle, because it is rather unjust to take seriously the Kaufman-Hart lines, in George Washington Slept Here, about summer theatre mummers; "So help me, actors will act anywhere and in anything; all they want to do is act." It is a good comedy line, but actually actors are not so unchoosy, especially where no salary is involved.

Kenneth Macgowan, analyzing in Footlights Across America the Little Theatre spirit as he sensed it some years ago, found in it a dominant motive:

"If you want to define it at its highest you call it the creative impulse. If you want to estimate it a little more realistically, if you want to risk looking at it in its lowest form, then you talk about a kind of exhibitionism. This desire to show off is an odd angle of a general human impulse to be doing something and doing something important."

I think most community actors will forgive Mr. Macgowan the word "exhibitionism" for the sake of the last sentence of that paragraph. Few amateurs would rather appear in a shoddy piece than play in Peer Gynt or Saint Joan. They really do prefer "doing something important." Even if "all they want to do is to act" they like to act in the best plays they can find.

The audience, next on Mr. Purdom's list, is reserved for a full treatment in a chapter all to itself. Finally, the practical considerations are entirely the director's problems and if the first three stipulations can be met there are few directors who will not find a way to overcome production difficulties sooner or later, one way or another.

Community theatres are, as a rule, far too anxious to produce plays which have enjoyed recent success in New York. The Samuel French office and the Dramatists' Play Service are invariably inundated with requests for releases as soon as each "hit" is established, and with unvarying tact and patience these agents continue to explain that even after a run has concluded on Broadway there may be clauses in the contract for the original production which will keep the script off the nonprofessional stages for several years. There is almost indecent impatience to do a "Best Play" the moment the release can be obtained. The reasons usually given for the urgency, namely, that the play will soon be out-of-date, or that everyone will have seen the movie version, seem to me the best possible arguments for leaving it alone. Surely only an occasional play is so ephemeral in its theme and treatment that it will not be equally acceptable five years later. Even Hollywood has discovered a box-office value in the re-filming of stories they used ten and fifteen years ago. And fifteen years is an eon in the celluloid cosmos.

Granville Barker refers to the drama's credit "built up over the years by the accumulation—and by time's selection—of a body of plays which have had in them an enduring worth and vitality." Very few indeed of the plays he had in mind have been shown on the community stages of America up to now. Mr. Burns Mantle is a distinguished critic and his annual volume provides an invaluable record of the current theatre in America, but he would hesitate, I feel sure, to put up many of his chosen plays against what Mr. Barker calls "time's selection."

At one time many observers of the new and vigorous "Little Theatre movement" hoped that its principal contribution would be the encouragement of new authors and through them the creation of a new American drama. That hope seems to have completely faded. The few even capable writers who had their first opportunity in the regional theatre and went from this into national prominence are the exceptions which prove this disheartening rule. There are so many other opportunities for a young writer with a flair for drama. Hollywood can always use him, Broadway will at least read his play and frequently buy an option on it for many times the amount that a provincial theatre could guarantee in the form of a royalty prize. The talented writer bypasses the regional theatre on his way to Broadway. The writer without talent may be encouraged by a local production but his play doesn't often help the local theatre, although some groups seem to have the idea that a play in manuscript should possess a special magical attraction for an audience, whatever its intrinsic value as drama.

There is one source of new material which has not received its fair share of attention, and that is the library of play literature made up of the hundreds of Broadway near-successes and even the actual "flops." The members of the Critics' Circle are not omniscient, and even if they were, there are many plays produced each year which do not do themselves justice in the few days of life allowed to them after the reviewers have done their worst. So many little things may have contributed to a weak presentation of what appeared to be a promising script. The direction may have been unimaginative, the casting at fault, the weather so bad that a mere handful of first-nighters made no effort to help the performers. Or perhaps, on the other hand, there were too many sympathizers and they tried too hard. At any rate the notices were lukewarm and the box office returns depressing, so another load of scenery went to Cain's warehouse, a handful of actors resumed their tour of the producers' offices, and one more embittered author put his script back again into the trunk.

Some of these plays were pretty bad, and perhaps the authors recognized that fact when they saw their work for the first time on the stage, but many of them should have had another chance. I can name twenty or more that come to mind, but to do so might be invidious. I prefer to generalize, which I can do with absolute confidence. Some few of these "Broadway flops"

I have since read in published form, because such shrewd judges as Garrett Leverton of Samuel French and Barrett Clark of Dramatists' Play Service perceived their value for the regional theatre even though New York would have little of them. Such plays as these are usually available long before the release of the "hits," but disappointingly few of them appear in the community repertories. Play selectors yearning for the latest thing would do well to give more consideration to these new and often arresting scripts.

French and Dramatists', and many others, will also be able to put local playreaders in touch with authors or producers of many other near-successes which have not been published. A play in typescript is still a play, and often a very good one. From the purely material point of view it is more advantageous for the community theatre to do a reproduction of a work which has sufficient merit to have justified the enormous expense of a Broadway showing than to take a chance on a completely new work merely because it can be programmed "for the first time on any stage."

Directors and playreaders alike should have more courage in their selections and not be so fearful of backing their judgment. It takes no special skill to read and approve *Life With Father, Harvey,* or *Arsenic and Old Lace,* but how many community playreaders, or even directors, took advantage of Maxwell Anderson's permission through the National Theatre Conference, to produce his *Truckline Cafe?* How many communities were favored by a production of *The Willow and I* until after *The Hasty Heart* had hoisted John Patrick to prominence and called attention to his earlier work?

At the present time the repertory of the average community theatre makes monotonous reading. The same "recent Broadway releases" make up about two-thirds of the schedule. What is there about that dull conformity to justify a claim to distinctive work? Are the play-selection committees exerting the dead hand, or is the director abusing his power of veto and stifling originality and experiment?

Following Mr. Purdom's formula we must presume that the directors are pleased, for they are still at their jobs. The same goes for the audience, because they keep on coming. Have the actors been heard from? Perhaps they might contribute something to an improvement in the situation, might relish the chance to know something of present-day writing other than in plays made too familiar by publicists, photographers, and gossip writers. Perhaps they might even like to dip into plays "of enduring worth and vitality" guaranteed by the selection of time and not by current magazines. I think they deserve the chance.

Who, then, does choose the plays? For his own peace of mind, I hope it is the director and that he has an absolutely free hand in the matter. It is his privilege and his responsibility not only because the theatre is his profession and his livelihood but because he is the sole authority by virtue of his appointment as director. He is able, through his training, his experience, and his absorption in his task to see the finished work on the stage in his mind's eye long before rehearsals start. The most devoted of amateur playreaders does not, cannot do this. If he (or she) could, they should be doing the directing. It is a matter of perspective, of seeing the completed picture in full detail, in imagination, before putting brush to canvas, and that is a task for the trained specialist, for the man who stakes his livelihood on his ability to achieve this perspective.

CHAPTER EIGHT

Cards on the Table

IT WOULD BE FOOLISH TO IGNORE THE POSSIBILITY OF SOME occasional misunderstandings. Differences of opinion are bound to arise among people keyed to high enthusiasms. There is likely to be no lack of outspoken comment, favorable or unfavorable, in an endeavor which frowns upon repressions and gives little encouragement to inhibitions. The theatre is a medium for self-expression, and if sufficient opportunities are not available in public performance it is not surprising if the pent-up energy finds an outlet in, so to speak, extracurricular channels.

The political leader is frequently able to silence an exceptionally vocal opponent by appointing him to a post of responsibility within the party machine. The theatre director cannot dispose of his critics so easily. There are just not enough leading roles to go around.

I use the word "misunderstanding" not with any idea of cynical understatement, but because inability to understand the other fellow's viewpoint is the root cause of all differences of opinion, whether between nations or individuals. The reason why a difference is allowed to continue and develop into a serious breach is that the proper measures for its removal are not taken early enough. A misapprehension becomes a grievance, and from this to a complete break in relations is only a matter of time. The cause of the misunderstanding should be removed as soon as the first difference of opinion arises.

Without going to the extent of proclaiming the inevitability of actual dissension we may as well face the fact that it may arise, as it does in even the happiest of relationships.

Most of the little discords within the theatre are usually microscopic in their beginnings. They would make the average marital disputation about bathroom precedence look like a case for the Supreme Court. But, while the majority of husbands and wives at least strive for agreement, the theatre disputants all too frequently thrive on vendetta.

Jealousy among the leading ladies may sometimes assume the proportions of a feud. The causes of the friction may be deep rooted and may not arise from any sins of omission nor commission on the director's part. If he finds himself on the side lines he is well advised to stay there. If, however, he has cast actress "A" in a role that was coveted by "B" he cannot remain aloof, and some explanation from him will be expected. Whatever his skill in the art of conference he will do well to offer the aggrieved lady more than honeyed words. The promise of an equally good part in the next production will be more productive than a wealth of explanation.

Honesty and frankness are recommended, but not to an extreme. For instance, very few theatres undertake to furnish, either by rental or borrowing, the women's wardrobe for a modern-dress production. If "X" is the best actress available for the lead in, for example, Lady In The Dark, but is known to have an inadequate wardrobe, then "Y," the lesser actress but possessed of the wealthier husband, may be awarded the role. In this case an over-frank statement of the reasons for passing "X" by would be cruel. The tactful director will find an explanation both adequate and kind.

Quite sizable vendettas may arise among the backstage contingent, particularly so in the department concerned with stage decoration. Possibly some perfectly appalling specimen of the genus bibelot may be brought in at the last minute. To the

A brusque rejection of the offering is quite justifiable

director, overwhelmed with anxieties and immersed in a sea of details, there is no time for a long explanation as to why the object in question is supremely unsuitable. Maybe a brusque rejection of the offering is quite justifiable, but this cavalier treatment will not be relished by the unfortunate volunteer who may have spent days tracking down her prize.

Of course with proper organization the director should never be reduced to such a condition of desperation. He should have his staff so organized that someone is responsible for the rejection of the unsuitable property. If the staff heads are capable they will themselves veto the unwanted trophy and so remove from the director the danger of incurring the lifelong emnity of some well-meaning contributor. Moreover, if the production staff is functioning according to plan these decorating problems will have been solved in good time and not allowed to become the subjects of last-minute decisions. Unfortunately the ideal setup does occasionally fail of realization, but at least the final dress rehearsal should start with everything in place, with nothing to be moved or changed from there on.

I have mentioned this adherence to a deadline as one of the stage manager's responsibilities. Apart from its value to the production in general, such adequate preparation will, believe me, remove many causes for small personal grievances, hurt feelings, and the other trifling seeds of a major dissension.

It should be remembered that the final rehearsals proceed in an almost violent crescendo, climaxing in the opening performance. Excitement is rising, temperament has full play, and hearts are being worn on sleeves. It is no time for anything but unanimity, for cooperation and harmony. Let the production workers—in every department—remember this and have their work finished and approved in good time. And let the director, too, be on his guard. Whatever his inner feelings, let him present to his little world an exterior of unruffled calm; however jangled his nerves, let him be ready only with the word of sympathy and approbation.

Even exercising what he believes to be supreme self-control

the director may, in the flurry and confusion of preparation, make a remark not calculated to improve amity, or he may even fail to say anything at all when some comment was expected. Unfortunately he is not always taken to task, in friendship and frankness, by the offended party nor does he have an intermediary who can salve wounded feelings before it is too late. Most of the time the director may be quite unconscious of having given offense and would actually value information about his shortcomings. He might well consider appointing a Keeper of His Conscience to notify him when some misapprehension has arisen, and tell him how it came about, so that he may remove the danger before it spreads.

To be unduly sensitive to the possibilities of discord would be to meet trouble halfway, which is as unproductive as the practice of digging up a plant every day to make sure the roots are still alive. There is no need for the director to assume that he is at fault whenever any disturbance arises, nor constantly to intervene in disputes that are not his concern, but if he actually does become involved or discovers that he has unwittingly given rise to a misapprehension of any kind he should act quickly for his own good and that of the theatre. He need not start off by offering to take the blame, but he ought to discover where it lies and spare no pains to restore harmony. An intelligent social instinct should prevent his carrying mea culpa to extremes.

These trivial injuries to feelings look very small in retrospect but they have a way of becoming magnified to grotesque proportions unless they receive prompt treatment. They may engender the gravest discord unless brought out into the open with explanations and apologies exchanged and accepted. If the suggestion does not sound too cynical, it might be wise to have a third party, the more influential and disinterested the better, present when these little smoke clouds are being cleared away. An unprejudiced witness to the ventilation may be valuable to prevent misquotation, which is why reconciliation by telephone is rarely satisfactory.

The members of the board of trustees may disagree violently but soon reconcile their differences because, as sensible people, they realize they have to go on working together. Their bickering is a private affair even though it takes place in a board meeting. It concerns no one but themselves; the theatre policy will eventually be decided by majority vote of the trustees. Two players may be at odds over some imagined stage discourtesy or selfish behavior in the dressing-room. If they don't stop feuding very promptly on their own initiative their fellow-actors will take a hand in the settlement. These little calamities are rarely of long life.

But when the director is a party to a dispute or is held responsible for some injury to feelings, real or imaginary, the outcome may be more serious. Perhaps it is one of the penalties of the certain kind of prominence which a theatre leader enjoys that his slightest word is recorded and repeated with amplification, and every nuance of his voice is capable of a hundred misinterpretations.

The art of conference is difficult in disputes involving the director because both parties (the director not being guiltless) frequently feel no urgent compulsion to settle the quarrel and resume normal fellowship. Both of the contestants far too frequently revel in their masochism and allow the grievance to fester and spread, ignoring the consequences to general morale. The amateurs, pursuing an avocation, may be permitted to nurse a grievance, but the professional, charged with the duty of maintaining morale and playing no favorites, must deny himself this luxury.

In addition to the perils of these small private affairs there is always the possible danger of a serious disagreement on policy. Even a contract which is specific in its outline of responsibilities may be in need of reinterpretation from time to time. In any case a theatre procedure should not be so inflexible as to admit of no adjustments or variations.

When a fundamental divergence of opinion on policy or procedure becomes evident the director's course is clear. He should lay the facts squarely before the board of trustees and unless he can persuade them to his point of view he should either accept their ruling with a good grace or tender his resignation.

When the board's ruling is in too violent conflict with his principles he has no option but to resign. If he persists in trying to administer the theatre in a way contrary to the expressed wishes of the trustees and in violation of the terms of his contract he should be given the opportunity to resign at the end of the current season. If he fails to take advantage of this face-saving device he should be notified that his services will not be required the following year. I know of at least one director who refused to resign and insisted upon the more drastic step being taken because, as he said, it would be a mark of distinction to be "fired" by such a group.

I cannot help believing that a few more of these compulsory "adjustments" would be healthy for the national picture. There are of course many theatres which have employed the same director for ten or more consecutive seasons. In some cases these men have set the indelible stamp of their personality upon the groups they lead and they would be difficult to replace. On the other hand there are many communities where the director, to put it quite charitably, has outlived his usefulness, has said all he has to say to that particular audience, and whose tenure is only secured by a constant series of compromises which militate against a really aggressive program for his theatre. His community needs a change and so does he. If he were to take his courage in both hands and indicate a desire to seek fresh fields he might discover much greater potentialities in new surroundings and among untried acquaintances.

The dangers of inertia are almost as great as those of discord. Complacency, whether on the part of the director or the governing body, is one of the deadly sins. There should be a more frequent reexamination of the theatre's position and at least an annual restatement of their respective aims by both parties to the contract. When it is discovered that they no longer see eye to eye, let them arrange an amicable parting of the ways with no hard feelings and the minimum of publicity. In that way both self-respect and mutual respect will be increased.

If the director is chafing under restrictions, but is unwilling to resign because of the possible disturbance to his domestic affairs or the fear of being unemployed, he is not functioning at the maximum of his efficiency. Neither is he being true to his ideals.

If the trustees are not getting what they want but are unwilling, because of consideration for an employee, to let him go—or if they coast along, preferring rather to bear the ills they have than fly to others that they know not of—then they are failing in their duty to their community.

There is no virtue in maintaining harmony, in keeping fences in repair, if the only objective is to retire behind a wall of complacency. Amity, friendly relations, and a smooth organization are only the means, never the end.

CHAPTER NINE

"Let Me Play the Lion, Too"

ONE OF THE LEAST STANDARDIZED OF PRODUCTION PROCEDURES is the selection of the cast. Many methods are in vogue, all of them attended by some degree of tribulation. The process of weeding out the unsuitable applicants is an anxious time for the players and very much of an ordeal for the director. He needs the courage of his convictions at this stage as at no other.

Governing all plans for the casting of a play is the fairly sound assumption that there will be more players than parts, that no one will need coaxing to undertake a role. There are exceptions to this state of affairs, but the rule is that most communities have only to hang out the sign "Casting Tonight" to have just about as many eager applicants as they can contain in the auditorium.

Moreover these volunteers will not always have the gift of seeing themselves as the director sees them; some of them will start the evening with their mind set on "Pyramus" and then see greater possibilities in "Thisbe" as the reading progresses. When there is no great surge of popular approval for their treatment of either part, they will be quick to offer to play the lion, too. Shakespeare could not possibly have foreseen the American community theatre, but Peter Quince lives over again in the person of every civic director who has to assemble a cast and make each member of it believe he has the most

"*Pyramus is a sweet-faced man.*"

effective role in the play. Present-day directors would do well to study Quince's methods of disciplining the temperamental Bottom: "You can play no other part but Pyramus; for Pyramus is a sweet-faced man; a proper man, as one shall see in a summer's day; a most lovely, gentleman-like man; therefore, you must needs play Pyramus."

Exquisite tact! And flattery none-too-subtle but mightily effective. Bottom and his posterity have never given another thought to the lion after a pep talk like that.

For reasons which will be discussed more fully later in this chapter we are assuming that the director has a completely free hand in the selection of his players. In this case his responsibility is to preserve the democratic processes, to make his choices openly and fearlessly, and to be entirely without prejudice against anything or anybody. His only consideration will be the best interests of the production.

The most widely used method is the public tryout. This is upheld as an expression of the democratic principle which will insure that all roles are awarded on merit as evidenced in fair competition. A public tryout is therefore required procedure for a theatre which preaches "wide participation." Any other method of allotting the roles would be repugnant to a group which proclaims a policy of opportunity for all.

Directors of theatres with more highly critical audiences will take the utmost pains to secure the most suitable cast by any and all means at their command. These directors may use the public tryout system with modifications. The two or three principal roles may perhaps be allotted some time previous to the public demonstration and when the general host of applicants appears these selected players may be called upon to read their assigned parts, while the unassigned roles are read around by the other members of the acting roster. Many directors feel that the presence of the more skilled players, especially after they have had a chance to spend time studying their parts, provides a great deal of inspiration for the less experienced readers.

A still nearer approach to the professional theatre's method, that of personal interview, is used by some directors. This is the custom of keeping very complete files on all their available players and then merely inviting the people they consider most suitable to make up the cast.

The successful working of any of these plans depends upon the temperament of the director and how shrewdly he can adapt himself to the local tradition established before his arrival. Whatever else he may desire to change, by methods direct or indirect, he is cautioned to proceed slowly with any alterations in the casting procedure. Any sudden application of revolutionary techniques in this department is likely to be fiercely resisted. An incoming director might have the green-room redecorated in pink, forbid all applause, and wear his hair in braids with much more safety than he could attempt to tamper with established custom in respect to casting the plays.

Back of the universally deep-rooted affection for the public tryout is the theory that all volunteers, as amateurs pursuing an avocation, must be treated alike, and that anyone who wishes to take part must submit to a competitive examination each and every time a play is to be cast. Recognized ability or previous achievement is not to be taken for granted or evaluated. Only those players who present themselves and take their chances are to receive consideration.

In theory, of course, this is a laudable idea, but it does not always succeed in practice because it takes no account of the "star" complex, which amiable human weakness is not confined to the professional stage. Many nonprofessional actors have a very real comprehension of their own talents, their drawing power, and their general indispensability. It is useless for the idealists to deplore such an "undemocratic" attitude on the part of their fellow citizens. It is foolish for the trustees to pass resolutions in order to dragoon the "stars" into compliance with their rules. Both director and trustees will be wise to accept the fact that this complex is pretty well universal and make the best of it.

I remember calling one very talented player to give him an

invitation to a tryout. Admittedly it was not his particular type of play and he knew it, but my idea was that such a skilled reader as he was might help to encourage some of the neophytes whom I expected to show up for the public reading. "Not on your life," said this veteran. "I know better ways to spend an evening than watching paralytics stumble around the stage and listening to illiterates ruining good dialogue." When I pointed out that I took a less pessimistic view of the evening's prospects he retorted: "Of course they will look different to you; it's your job to put up with that kind of thing. You know what I can do. When you have a part you really want me to play, call me up and I promise you I'll do it."

He was not the only player in that city who took that attitude. I discovered that the "star" system had been sanctioned by usage and tradition, and the realistic thing for me to do was to accept it, plan accordingly, and endeavor by patience and subtlety to bring about some change in the course of time. The players who took this stand were not "choosy"; they really trusted my judgment, and none of them ever refused a proffered part all the time I was there. But they would not come to tryouts of the kind I had planned. Their resistance was eventually broken down by the adoption of the modified procedure, that is, of having the selected leads read with the general body of applicants.

If public readings are conducted according to the letter of a broadly democratic plan the business of casting may take a long time. Seventy-five or a hundred people cannot be given a fair hearing in one session. Some of them will have to be asked to return the following evening and the winnowing process may go on for days. Yet the plan can only be regarded as successful in principle and practice if the public readings are attended by overwhelming numbers, by "the full strength of the company" as the old melodrama playbills expressed it.

Of course the attendance at the public readings is never as complete as the record of available players would indicate. The first turnout of the season, particularly when there is a new director, may overflow the auditorium, but tryout attendance will taper off to a trickle during the year. It would severely handicap the director if he had to make his selection only from those who presented themselves and ignore both the "stars" and the diffident ones who stayed away. The logical but completely unthinkable conclusion of such a policy would be that the season would invariably open with something on the scale of *Street Scene* and end, after a rapid diminuendo in the size of the casts, with *Jealousy* or even a monodrama.

The second plan—the modification of the open reading— does not offend the community spirit nor deprive the talented beginner of an opportunity. It is practical because the director, with perhaps less than four weeks in which to rehearse a play, protects himself by making sure that two or three of his most skilled players are available for the leading roles and even by having discussed the interpretation with the actors before asking them to lead the public readings.

This question of availability is important. If the entire season's repertory has been chosen in advance, the director can negotiate with the key players and have some assurance that they will be willing to play this or that part, moreover that their business or domestic obligations will not interfere with concentration on rehearsals. Happily married leading ladies are apt to have periodical additions to their families; popular young businessmen will attend conventions or have to make out-of-town trips on more prosaic business; even the character actors have their own private lives. The more valuable a player the greater are the chances that he or she is also a busy citizen involved in a dozen or more civic and personal enterprises which make conflicting demands upon time and energies. With these people the theatre does not always come first.

Under this second plan the director will have offered the more important parts to the best available players some weeks ahead of the public reading, will have discussed and analyzed the characterizations, and urged the actors to start memorizing if need be. He will then ask them to attend the tryout and make no secret of the fact that they are to play certain roles. This is preferable, in my opinion, to allowing the less experienced aspirants to struggle with parts beyond their range and it will permit them, instead, to concentrate upon characterizing the roles they have more chance of playing. It also prevents disappointment, as the anticipations of these young players are not so likely to be dashed to the ground.

There will not be unanimous agreement with this suggested procedure. Some directors believe that the beginners will show to greater advantage in reading for roles that are manifestly beyond their powers or experience, that offer them a challenge. These directors will allow the self-conscious ingénue to read a big scene opposite the player already cast in the leading male part, or ask the hesitant juvenile to try a love scene with the local Cornell. Sometimes the tyros rise to the occasion, but much more frequently they don't, and in the meantime the minutes are fleeting, the schedule is inexorable, and the director is impatient to complete the cast and get to work.

The third method in frankly autocratic, but is perhaps the only possible one for a director operating on a "tight schedule." The director knows the available acting strength of his group, negotiates with the people he considers best suited, and calls the cast together. This sounds easy—autocracy always seems simple—but to rely solely upon such a plan the director must possess an up-to-the-minute filing system, a long memory, some intuitive genius, and the complete confidence of his trustees, to say nothing of a saintly humility when fading stars, passed over in the shuffle, begin to attack him.

As an adjunct to all these methods some form of personal interview or private reading is often desirable. In the professional theatre such a method is used almost exclusively. In a personal interview an atmosphere of ease and informality can be created while the play is discussed and the player encouraged to make his or her contribution. If these interviews take place in the director's office or in a rehearsal room where the actors can move around they will not be so self-conscious about

Fading stars . . . begin to attack him

emotional expression. This intimate drawing-out of the player is impossible in a public tryout where only the highly experienced player will be sufficiently free of inhibitions to deliver a convincing reading, and the chances are that such glibness may well represent the full extent of that performer's powers. Many amateurs do their best work at a first reading and never even equal it in actual performance.

Some good readers of my acquaintance must be excused from this sweeping indictment. They profess to like the atmosphere of a public reading, are inspired by the presence of even a ragged audience of sympathizers and competitors, and prefer to make their bid in this way rather than through individual private interviews. They vote for a compromise whereby the director would call together a skeleton cast and let them read together. Possibly the players would switch parts many times in the course of the evening, but always they would draw a great deal of inspiration from the interplay with their equally competent opposites. Such a procedure as this is frequently adopted by those directors who omit the public reading. Arbitrary first choices may prove to be unsatisfactory when viewed in relation to the other players, and it is well to delay announcement of the final selection until a few of these tentative readings have been held. It is much easier to relieve a player during this probationary period than after the play is in movement, and the few days spent in this trial process cannot be regarded as wasted because each meeting serves to clarify the director's plan for the characterizations and to familiarize the real nucleus of the cast with the play's content.

If changes have to be made, especially after rehearsals are well under way, the unsatisfactory player must be relieved of his part in a manner that will not damage his self-respect. Even the most temperamental actors are basically unselfish and reasonable if they are satisfied that the director is acting in their best interests and is himself unselfish. There is no need for elaborate prevarication. An honest appreciation of the actor's effort to succeed in his task, and a confession that the director's judgment has been at fault is the best way. The parting of the ways must come with perfect friendliness and both sides must be in agreement that the best course is being pursued. The director should then find the right part for the displaced player at the first possible opportunity, preferably in the following production. I would recommend that after such a painful necessity as the requested resignation of a player the director explain the circumstances to the entire cast, giving due credit to the removed actor, praising his sporting attitude and asking for sympathetic co-operation with the new player who has stepped into the breach. If another member of the cast has to be dropped either from this or any subsequent production he will accept his dismissal with a better grace when he recalls the dignified style of these proceedings. Above all, no director should ever be guilty of expressing satisfaction at having rid himself of a poor actor or a bad trouper. The reason given, in public and in private, must always be the welfare of the play and nothing else.

The occasional necessity for dropping a player is the final argument against the practice of casting by a committee. Actors much prefer their selection to be the result of a professional estimate of their ability. Conversely they will accept their congé much more cheerfully from the director than at the hands of a group of their fellow members. It would be insupportable for a committee to select and the director to reject, or vice versa. The possibilities of such a tangle of conflicting authorities are too appalling to contemplate.

To put it quite bluntly, hiring and firing must be in the hands of the one competent authority. The director's back is broad enough to carry this burden without any help.

On the other hand, a committee which would operate to assist the director in the discovery of new players, urging them to attend tryouts or to make appointments with the director for a private reading, is of immense value. The members of such a committee can provide an atmosphere of hospitality at the public readings, greeting newcomers, persuading the bashful ones to come forward, recording names and addresses and perhaps giving the director the benefit of their impressions when the reading is over. Every director will be appreciative of such help. He, himself, will need to give undivided attention to the people who are reading, and even though he is the soul of courtesy he cannot interrupt this concentration to make small talk with every late arrival, whether an invaluable veteran or a promising newcomer. He will, naturally, want to meet personally all who attend, but only at a time when the happenings on the stage do not demand his watchful eye and attentive ear.

Proper organization of the tryout sessions along these lines will do much to mitigate the suspense and anguish which is often attendant upon such occasions. When Viola said "what is yours to bestow is not yours to reserve" she might well have been thinking of the casting authority. The director, who usually takes quite seriously his responsibility of omnipotence in the bestowal of roles, should always act graciously in the withholding of opportunities. It is just as important to "reserve" as it is to bestow, and failure to do so with the proper dignity is a dereliction of duty.

A director should never forget that for some of the neophytes it has taken a supreme summoning-up of courage to present themselves at all. Also, for many experienced players a tryout is an ordeal which never fails to produce queasiness and mental distress. But these veterans know that it takes supreme self-confidence to be an actor of any kind. Butterflies-in-the-stomach is an occupational disease much more common on Broadway than on Main Street, but professionals have learned to brace themselves, to rise above such involuntary nervous annoyances. However terrifying the atmosphere of a tryout to the sensitive soul, it is as nothing compared to the anguish of an opening night. The nonprofessional must learn to give a good account of himself under any circumstances and the tryout is a good time to begin.

Most community theatres are at present enjoying unexampled prosperity and are playing almost twice the number of performances they presented five years ago. A schedule predicated on a week's run, followed by a week of tryouts and interviews and three weeks of intensive rehearsal used to space the opening of the seven productions about five weeks apart. Nowadays the plays are running two weeks or even longer in many cases, and three weeks is still the absolute minimum for adequate rehearsal. Casting for the subsequent play must be done during the run of the current one and, as few groups possess any rehearsal accommodation other than their auditorium, rehearsals cannot start until each production has closed. Three or four days spent in readings and interviews will upset the delicate balance of this timetable, the productions will be under-rehearsed and standards will suffer.

Some theatres have solved this problem by reducing the number of productions, from eight to seven, seven to six, and so on. As far as my information goes they have not lowered their subscription price, and this increase in the pro-rata cost of their admissions has not been resented by the membership who willingly make this contribution to rising production costs. The reduced schedule gives the director more time to cast and rehearse each production and so maintain his standards.

Directors of other theatres have discovered ways to pay homage to the principle of general tryouts without allowing it to delay their timetable. One highly practical scheme begins with a high pressure campaign to invite every possible player to a series of tryouts before the season begins. At these sessions no particular play is read, but the applicants, particularly if they claim little or no experience, are encouraged to take part in improvisations and to read effective scenes from a varied assortment of plays. The committee assisting the director makes a very complete record of their achievements in these parts, and unless the director plans to cast them in the first play, invites them to come back at a later date.

This group, usually of younger people but not by any means

exclusively so, becomes the Workshop Group, and either the Assistant Director (if there is a professional staff member performing these duties) or some of the experienced players around the theatre will undertake to direct them in some one-act plays. Sometimes they will serve as understudies for the main cast and perform the play themselves for an invited audience during or immediately after the regular run. They will have the benefit of the actual scenery, props and lights, and the backing of the regular stage crew, all of which factors help them to a better exhibition of their powers than if they performed in an improvised production. The director has an opportunity to see them in rehearsed roles, whether doubling in the three-act play or in their own "one-acters," they have an audience to provide inspiration, and their enthusiasm is not allowed to languish.

After the pre-season welter of tryouts—it may well occupy every evening of a week or more—no further public readings will be held, but the director will be able to cast his major productions from his list of tried and experienced players, plus any promotions from the Workshop Group as a result of performances which have impressed him. People who were out of town when the tryout festival was held, or those who move in from other cities during the season will find a way to make themselves known to the director in some way or other. If they are willing and able they will have no need of the announcement of a public reading to encourage them to come forward.

Whatever method is used, whichever the type of theatre concerned, the director alone can be the judge of the player's capabilities and his fitness for the role under consideration. Most experienced practitioners develop a sixth sense for this exercise of judgment. With Stark Young (in The Flower in Drama), they feel that: "To those who have an eye for it, Talent is discernible at once when it comes on the stage; it establishes a kind of luminosity of the presence, a radiance of the body seen to be living out the moment there . . . Talent is inexpressible, like all natural things. It is its own description."

The experienced director has to "have an eye for it," and although Mr. Young was speaking of talent observed in performance the attribute is either there or it isn't, and it is usually observable at the first glance, at the first hearing.

Usually, that is to say, but not always. It is dangerous to trust the sixth sense too implicitly. Too many directors, forgetting that it is impossible to make bricks without straw, are overconfident about their ability to create the required characterizations out of unpromising material. But the power of a strong personality cannot be disputed, and unless the productions are to be merely competent and colorless, the director will seize on the players who "come over the footlights" at a first reading and pray for more like them. They will be harder to handle than the mild-mannered and more easily molded ones of moderate ability. They may overdo the subjective approach when an objective one would better suit the part, but they can, and do, bring the play to life and inspire their fellow players to their best efforts.

The community theatre players of my experience have been very fine people. They have always cheerfully accepted the necessity for stage discipline, they have placed themselves freely under direction, and offered themselves for the good of the production as a whole. They have been devoted, loyal, and deserving of the best efforts of their director. The players' devotion places their leader under an obligation which he can discharge only by making the most honorable use of it.

CHAPTER TEN

The Unsung Heroes

〰〰

I CAN THINK OF NO GROUP OF HUMAN BEINGS WHOSE ENTHUSI-asms accord less with rationality and common sense than the backstage workers. Why they should prefer grimy hands and faces, paint-stained overalls and a sixteen-hour working day to the ordinary amenities of a leisure-conscious age is a problem for psychologists. Their behavior is the more fantastic when we remember that the vast majority of these irrational beings receive no financial return for their labor and none of the acclaim that the actors accept in lieu of little or no salary.

Girls who at home cannot be bribed into picking up their own clothes, husbands who send for the electrician to replace a blown fuse, wives who leave their husbands' socks undarned will cheerfully respond to a crew call, do the filthiest jobs, wrestle successfully with complicated technical details, and religiously "police" their working area before crawling home to bed in the small hours.

To the solid, respectable, and rational citizen such behavior indicates a more than mild form of insanity. Even to the actors, at least to those of them who are at all conscious of backstage proceedings, the zeal of the painters and carpenters is quite incomprehensible. The actor looks forward to the reward of applause for his contribution; he supposes that the members of the crew must be somehow enjoying themselves

103

A more than mild form of insanity

and he is not openly contemptuous, but he views their antics with a sort of Olympian tolerance.

The backstage technicians, for their part, cannot fathom the mentality of people who nightly repeat nonsense over and over, paint their faces, wear grotesque clothing, and then strut and bellow in full view of an audience which has obviously come with no other purpose than to admire the scenery and marvel at the lighting. The members of the crew are in no need of the actor's pity or tolerance; they are completely happy in their own little world of make-believe.

In any theatre group there may be one or two unique specimens who are both player and painter, actor and artisan, and who like to ring the changes on their enthusiasms. But these ambidextrous types lack the full potentiality of either classification. They are too well adjusted with their sense of proportion too well preserved. The exhibitionist actor and the fanatical crewman live in two separate worlds.

The director of any community theatre owes more to these zealots backstage than he is usually willing to admit. Their amazing devotion to the job, coupled with an unswerving conviction of the paramount importance of their work, is a factor in successful operation quite unrecognized by the majority of the audience and far too frequently, also, by the man who receives most of the credit for a good production.

Without proper recognition of some kind the continuing enthusiasm of the crew-workers cannot be taken for granted. Nor, indeed, should it be. The cold-blooded attitude that the backstage gang will work anyway, for anything, for anybody, is both inhuman and unintelligent. Even the most fanatical of them will work more zealously on a good play than on a bad one, will do their best work on a production that gives scope to them as well as to the actors, and they will break their backs for a director who realizes his indebtedness to them and is generous enough to give it expression.

Unfortunately not a few directors are confessedly quite ignorant of the technical side of production. They either manage to engage a capable professional technician and hold him responsible for all details, or they assume what they believe to be a lovable attitude of helplessness and trust to the pity of their volunteer helpers to overcome all the problems. Specimens of this latter type were by no means uncommon in the early days of the Little Theatre movement, and the success of their tactics was the marvel of their more practical, but less subtle, professional brethren.

This fading-lily type of director belongs to a vanishing breed. The drama departments of colleges and universities now turn out skilled people with a well-rounded education in all branches of production. Competition is too keen for any applicant to be able to shrug off inquiries about his technical knowledge with the airy suggestion that such matters are beneath his consideration. Even if he never has to wet a paintbrush or throw a light switch he must know how—and why—in order to command the respect of his volunteers.

If the theatre staff includes a professional aide, whether titled assistant director, technical director, or technician, this official will head the crew activities, and the volunteers will look to him rather than to the director himself for inspiration and leadership. It might even cause some resentment for the director, in this case, to have too much individual contact with the members of the production crew. Most technicians prefer to manage their own work and to direct the operations of their volunteer helpers without the embarrassing presence of "the head man." They may suspect that they are being observed with a critical eye and that their authority is being subtly undermined. It is well to give them no cause for suspicion even at the cost of some personal feeling of frustration.

Most technicians are recent graduates of drama schools and therefore of a comparable age with the majority of the volunteers they supervise. The director himself may be anxious to avoid the pedagogical attitude, but if he is a man of mature years he will place the members of the crew *in statu pupillari* in spite of all he can do. It is more satisfactory for the crew leader to function as counsellor rather than as professor.

A responsibility then devolves upon the assistant, the counsellor, to exhibit the same loyalty to his chief that he expects from the volunteers. This is a relationship between two professionals who have everything to gain by a proper understanding and mutual respect and so much to lose by disagreement or jealousy.

But the director will do himself no good if he affects superiority and the attitude that no matter who sweeps the stage his own hands must not be soiled. If he is like most of my professional friends, he will feel nostalgia for his own days with the crew, and angle for an occasional invitation to join the painters or the carpenters at their jobs. He will wisely esteem such an invitation as a privilege and one not to be abused by an air of patronage or condescension.

The young director, with no professional assistance and an untrained backstage organization, must be prepared to direct, instruct, and take part in the work of production, and it is in such cases that the valor and zeal of the backstage heroes gains his real appreciation. The director who inherits an adequate staff and a smooth-running backstage misses a great deal.

The arduous and frequently unpleasant jobs around a production are cheerfully undertaken only when the proper spirit of teamwork prevails. There can be no star system here, with one to paint and the other to wash out the bucket; artists must be good housekeepers as well as good troupers. Competition is at a discount and co-operation is the legal tender.

The American genius for improvisation here finds full play. This is the artistic release which may explain the sometimes extraordinary achievements of these crew-workers. I recoil with distaste from the term "occupational therapy" as applied to work backstage. The theatre still has a bad enough reputation in some puritanical quarters without openly avowing discipleship with the original Therapist who still finds occupation for idle hands.

Whatever the original compulsion, most people who join a stage crew do not stay with it because it gives them some place to go. Instead, they have joined a rather select brotherhood and they are jealous of their privileges. They will resent the casual helper, the occasional curious visitor, and any new ad-herent must present ample evidence of worthiness and a will-ingness to stick it out.

The director, or his technical assistant, will recognize the possessive pride which the regular crew-worker has for his job and his tools. It is not politic to allow the backstage to become a closed corporation but, except in very special cases, it is un-desirable to allow newcomers to join the crew after production is under way. Some directors take a very firm stand and allow no new members to join this very exclusive club after the first play of the season. This seems to be taking unnecessary risks because the genuine fanatics are never too numerous. There are always fifty would-be actors for every one who will be supremely happy in the paint bucket or the nail box. Exclusive-ness should stop short of actual exclusion.

For this reason it is well to publicize the early crew sessions each season and even glamorize them in order to attract the largest number of potential workers. For a few evenings there may be more than twice as many hands as hammers, and very little work accomplished. This can be foreseen and prepared for; the timetable will make allowance for a slow start.

Some of the visitors will never reappear, others may come three or four times before finally dropping out of sight. The remainder will be the cream of the new crop, the loyal appren-tices who by the time three plays have been mounted have become journeymen in one or another of the crafts. Next sea-son, if they have been properly indoctrinated, they will be able to head departments, coach new workers and quite justifiably resent the curiosity seeker, the dilettante, and the ones who can't take it.

Up to this point I have seemed to suggest that the hammer and the paintbrush are the only tools used backstage. I should add the gluepot, the pliers and the friction tape, the needle and the electric iron. I have many grateful memories of a team of four young women who volunteered as "wardrobe aides." Working in shifts of their own arrangement for the whole season, they did a monumental job. Every afternoon two of them would press the costumes, every evening the other two would be on hand an hour before curtain time with needles poised to repair the ravages of the previous night's frenzies. After every exit they gently but firmly escorted the excitable grande dame or the hairbrained ingénue to the dressing rooms, removed their dresses and hung them safely out of reach. They were dressers, ladies' maids, valets—asking no pay and receiving scant recognition.

The normal, sane members of the audience will wonder what possible inducement is offered for girls to undertake such "menial" duties, or what compels the "prop" girls to go down night after night and arrange a lot of very second-rate-looking bric-à-brac on the stage and then stand motionless in a dark corner holding a wallet, a bouquet, or a telegram for some actor to snatch from her hands without even a whispered word of thanks. Or—to stay half an hour or more after the audience and most of the cast have left the building, washing cups, plates and glasses, and perhaps boiling water to make the tea that tomorrow night will masquerade as whisky, wine, brandy, or even—tea.

An efficient and conscientious property mistress will have nothing to do with tricks and practical jokes. There can be only pity for the infantile sense of humor which prompts the exploding cigar, the burnt cork on the telephone earpiece, or the doctored stage drink. I am never very amused when told of how so-and-so found himself drinking the real thing on the last night of the play, and I'm sure the actor was not. He would have enjoyed his little tipple much more a few minutes later, across the street, after the play was over. And the audience, who paid just as much for their seats that night as for any other, were entitled to see just as good a performance as on any other night. Even the minutest quantity of alcohol will wreak havoc with an actor's memory at an unexpected moment, or slow up his reactions enough to disturb his control and impair his performance. The time for "Dutch courage" is after the curtain is down, not during or even just before the play.

I can recall only one occasion when "Props" exhibited a warped sense of humor, and I remember that no reproof of mine was needed. She made the mistake of spiking a whole tray of "cocktails," and seven very angry players (including two lifelong abstainers) came storming off the stage in turn to make sure that trick would never be repeated. I made the discovery that evening that temperance in the matter of alcohol does not always imply temperance in language. For the misguided property mistress that incident was the end of several beautiful friendships.

Such juvenilities as this are the worst kind of amateurism, and the director who encourages or even permits them is far more guilty than the actual perpetrators. Of course the alleged jokes make good anecdotes, enjoyed by all but the victims, but viewed from the audience point of view, they are a breach of faith.

The fact that some professionals have been guilty of similar bad taste makes it no more excusable. The story of Caruso nailing to the floor a glove which Scotti had to discover on his entrance, pick up, and kiss in simulated rapture, is frequently told as justification for imitative pranks in the amateur theatre. One should not forget that the glove incident took place on the operatic stage, where one more absurdity could make little difference. There will be plenty of ludicrous happenings in the legitimate theatre, amateur or professional, without any adolescents going out of their way to manufacture them.

The most spectacular contributions to the production come from the volunteers who design and paint the settings, dress them with furniture and draperies, and provide the lighting which gives the final touch of glamor. The workers in these departments have a more obvious opportunity for self-expression. Indeed, they may even become too individual, and the

director will need all his tact and resolution to prevent the
play's being smothered under a confusion of detail.

He will need to have complete confidence in the good taste
and co-operative spirit of the people who have to be blended to
make a functioning productive machine. That is why it is important that he have a voice in the selection of the team
which is to work on each play.

A local architect may frequently be induced to lend his
talent by designing an interior. His proportions may be impeccable, the detail perfect, but the floor plan may possibly be
unexciting. The director will have to explain the demands of
the play and point out the limitations as well as the license of
the stage. He must do this without reducing the zest of the
architect, who possibly thought three walls would be easier
than four.

The "décor committee" can be either a joy forever or an
abiding menace. My own personal experience includes both
extremes, but it does include the privilege of working with at
least three very gifted and stage-wise decorators, who appreciated the difference between furnishing a room and dressing a
set. They perceived the angle from which the set is viewed,
which in a dwelling would be equivalent to lying on a hearth
rug and letting the eye travel up from the baseboard to the top
of the chairs. They knew that since few communities have
balconies in their playhouses, the under side of the furniture is
sometimes more important than the top, and that the way to
check on their work was to view it from the center of the
auditorium and not from a standing position on the stage.

Most valuable of all, they never lost sight of the fact that
they were dressing the set as the background for a play. They
realized that their work was to be viewed from a distance and
not subjected to microscopic examination at close range. It
was a deliberate attempt at successful illusion, not an exhibit
at the Metropolitan Museum. To them a blurred smear of
appropriate color framed in cardboard could be made to pass,
at twenty paces, for an Old Master, and would be actually

more appropriate than an irreplaceable borrowed heirloom. They had learned, moreover, that the frankly theatrical picture might be suspended from just a tack in the scene wall, moved by one hand when the quick change had to be made, and rehung with the same ease. They had discovered, too, that paper flowers when they are good of their kind, will satisfy everyone but the busybodies who come onstage after the show to smell them; that artificial flowers stay fresh during the run of the show, need no water and therefore cannot be upset on a satin-velvet sofa.

This latter catastrophe actually happened to a stage decorator of the realistic school. The sofa, a borrowed piece from his own shop, had to be re-covered at a cost of over a hundred dollars and after that experience the decorator became a strong believer in the art and practice of illusion.

Most community theatre settings are too cluttered, and so knee-deep in knickknacks and extraneous pieces that the players are obviously terrified to move around. There has been some improvement in recent years, but there are still too many productions which place too much reliance upon a startling décor and too little upon the acting which should be the primary attraction for the audience.

Between the Spartan simplicity of the rehearsal setup—two chairs, a bench, and a table—and the almost Babylonian excesses of the final setting, there is an unexplored region of possibilities. Instead of trying to find space for one more picture, one more vase, the object of the décor committee (or the art director) should be to discover just how few items need be used to gain the proper effect. The characters on the stage should not be deprived of any essential properties, and the setting need not be so bare that the audience gets the impression that the stage family has been in arrears with its payments on the furniture.

The stage manager and his functions belong in any consideration of backstage work. In the professional theatre he or his assistant is at the director's elbow from the first rehearsal. In the community enterprise he usually rebels at having to attend so often, and since his principal contribution will be made during the run of the play he will try to persuade the director to a compromise. My own practice was to ask the stage manager to the first reading, discuss the production problems with him, and obtain his promise to study the script at his leisure and be prepared to function regularly about a week before the first dress rehearsal. If he is capable and experienced, this is ample time for him to establish a routine; if he is not, then someone else should be doing his job.

Planning the early stages of the production timetable is the director's task. As the work goes on, responsibility for its progress will depend upon the assistant, the technical director. By the time the technical rehearsal is due the stage manager should be prepared to take over.

Sometimes the limitations of a nonprofessional plant make it impossible to hold the three full-scale rehearsals that are needed to insure a well-prepared opening. But if only one dress rehearsal is possible, it should be preceded by a very complete "technical" at which the cues for curtains, lights, entrances, and exits may be well rehearsed and the stage manager can begin to gather into his hands the threads of control.

It should not be necessary to dwell on the vital necessity of making the fewest possible changes in any branch of the production between the end of the technical rehearsal and the opening performance. A good stage manager will relieve the director of much anxiety if he insists upon everything's being in place at least two days before the audience is expected. To permit the properties department to make last-minute changes is to hazard the smooth running of the performance; actors are frequently panic-stricken on discovering a strange sofa or a different-sized doorknob. At the dress rehearsals they suffer enough, but they should be able to accustom themselves to the furniture when no audience is present and then make their entrance into completely familiar surroundings on the opening night.

This is necessarily a counsel of perfection. The exact piece of furniture required may not be obtainable until the last minute, or there may be other valid reasons why the decorator or the property mistress have to take what they can, when they can. But if all backstage departments would think of their deadline as being no later than the first dress rehearsal, there would be fewer first-nights marred by awkward occurrences.

It is the stage manager's province to goad the workers to a realization of this fact, and for his own peace of mind if not for that of the director's or the players', to see that the machine he has to run for seven, ten, twelve, or even twenty performances is well oiled and efficient.

CHAPTER ELEVEN

A Still Small Voice

MANY OF THE TRADITIONAL DUTIES OF THE STAGE MANAGER ARE now undertaken by the prompter. This invaluable person is usually appointed even before the cast is selected and from then on is expected to attend every rehearsal, recording all the moves and the stage business and preparing to assert the authority of the script.

The prompter, by that title, and functioning in this way, is a phenomenon peculiar to the nonprofessional theatre. She is more than assistant stage manager, because she works more closely with the director in the rehearsing of the play. Without the authority of an assistant director and having no responsibility for the actual art of directing, she has an opportunity to learn much about the craft. She controls the mechanics by which the director's art is realized, and while his work is, in theory, finished with the final dress rehearsal, the prompter's most spectacular duties still lie ahead.

During the preparation period she assumes the stage manager's role by laying out the floor plan, arranging the rehearsal furniture and calling the players for each scene as well as holding the book. This is the new tradition, perhaps brought about by the fact that the stage manager and his assistant are also good technicians and may need to spend their evenings constructing a set or repairing the switchboard.

There are many reasons to justify the choice of a woman for the job of prompter. She will possess the necessary qualities of patience, and her voice, if it ever has to be heard during performance, will be less obtrusive than a man's. Also, she will be a well-prepared substitute for any of the women players who might be unable to appear at the last moment, with the director himself being in readiness to step into any of the male roles similarly vacant. Understudies, as such, are not practical politics in any but a professional company. The director and his assistant, the prompter, can usually cope with the average-sized emergency in the community theatre.

Until such an occasion arises and finds the prompter prepared to close the breach, she rarely receives full credit for her loyalty and devotion. However grateful to her the players may be for a whispered cue in a "line-blank" they are apt to regard her insistence on the use of the author's exact words in rehearsal as a personal insult. She has to be either a supremely patient soul with a quiet tenacity or a dogmatic disciplinarian with the hide of a rhinoceros.

Many directors pay tribute to the importance of the prompter by listing her as Assistant to the Director. This has a dignified ring and quite truthfully expresses the relationship. It is quite different from the title and responsibility of Assistant Director. To list her as Prompter or Book-holder is quite inadequate, while to omit her name altogether on the grounds that the audience (if they read that part of the program) must not be encouraged to believe that prompting is ever needed, is the purest self-deception.

It is equally unrealistic to have no prompter on hand during the performances, which is the practice of some few directors. This is a form of deviltry which cannot possibly be relished by the players. Accidents will happen, the memories of even highly skilled professionals will fail on occasion, and there can be nothing more productive of anguish than to know that when the line-blank comes there is nothing to do but flounder around until inspiration returns.

A friend of mine who was a member of the audience when the incident occurred, tells a story of a community theatre performance under the "no-prompter" rule. The director did not believe in his players having to rely upon the book, and once the curtain was up, left them to sink or swim.

On this particular evening a long speech was in progress when the actor's memory failed him about halfway through. He paused, gazed wildly around, and, realizing that no help would be forthcoming, took a breath and went back again to the beginning. At the same place again he came to a full stop, and after an even more despairing survey of the unresponsive scenery he repeated the process, back again to the start. My informant swears that the audience heard the first part of that long speech five times, before someone finally walked on and threw in an impromptu line which the miserable sufferer seized to pull himself to safety.

The actor's agony can well be imagined, but the audience endured a great deal. For the sake of an impractical principle, was it worth subjecting several hundred people to acute embarrassment? And what happened to the play in the meantime?

It is undeniable that a well-drilled cast will seldom need a prompter's voice, but the knowledge that there is someone watching the book, and doing so efficiently, will give any player a feeling of security and confidence. The audience, too, will prefer to know that such a functionary as the prompter is in attendance. Although many movie patrons have the quaint idea that their gods and goddesses speak extempore, being especially gifted that way, theatre audiences are not so naïve. They know that the actor has to memorize, and they know, also, that someone has to function as a lifeguard in case the player has cramps in his vocabulary or gets out of his verbal depth.

Much as the audience dislikes hearing the prompter's voice at a performance, they prefer this assurance that the situation is remediable to the prospect of an awkward and embarrassing silence or the recognizable symptoms of panic as exhibited by inexpert improvising or senseless repetition of lines in the hope of inspiration. Speaking for myself, as a member of the audience I prefer the author's lines, neither garbled nor repeated ad nauseam, and as a director I prefer the security which a good prompter can provide. As an actor I prefer the still small voice to the babble of frenzied ad-libbing.

Professional practice, with the duties of book-holding delegated to the assistant stage manager, leaves the stage manager himself free to move around and exercise the fullest supervision. There will sometimes be two complete and identical scripts, one held by each of these two officials, and the stage manager may himself execute the required offstage noises such as phone bells, door knocks, gunshots, and the chiming of clocks, or he may signal them to the crew member responsible for their actual execution.

In the community organization, especially if the stage manager does not attend all rehearsals, the prompter will be answerable for supplying all these effects on time. Her script will show all the cues and she will know, for instance, from painful experience at rehearsals, that "X" never makes his entrance or picks up the telephone on exactly the same word every night, or that "Y" has to be carefully watched because she is erratic in her setting of the table and sometimes has the job unfinished when the doorbell has to ring. From her position in the wings, the prompter can see the stage and the players and so can co-ordinate the dialogue, action, and sound to a nicety.

Prompters should preferably be tiny, they should certainly not be limbed like Atalanta. They frequently have to huddle, coiled like a pretzel, in the shadow of the proscenium arch, or crouch in a fireplace or outside a window in order to see the stage. Under such circumstances length of limb is a positive disadvantage. One eye must be always on the script, the other on the stage, and vigilance cannot be relaxed for a moment, though the heavens fall.

They frequently have to crouch in a fireplace

One faithful assistant of mine saw the curtain safely down one night on the second act and then collapsed in a very authentic faint. When she had been restored she told how a mouse had been playing around her feet for the last ten minutes of the act. Another devotee sprained her ankle coming in the stage door on opening night, but insisted on taking her place as usual. A doctor was pried out of his seat in the audience just as the curtain was going up, applied bandages in the shadowy prompt corner while the first act was being played, and the property man managed to unearth a pair of crutches for the plucky girl to navigate with. She held the book for the entire run of the show, over my protests, which were really quite feeble since I knew she was happier staying with the show than moping at home. But her mother took a long time to forgive me for my slavery tactics, as she called them.

The lesser occupational hazards connected with assisting the director will include cramped limbs, barked shins, and colds in the head occasioned from sitting in draughty corners. The life is full of incident as well as of hazard, and at least one director has been known to fall in love with and marry his prompter. This phenomenon might be classified as an occupational hazard with a low percentage of incidence. All directors become very attached to these loyal souls who metaphorically hold their hands as well as the script, some grow very fond indeed of them, but few are able, on account of prior obligations, to offer matrimony as an expression of their gratitude.

CHAPTER TWELVE

Misfits and Misapprehensions

"PARKING PLACE FOR WIVES" WAS THE TERM FREQUENTLY applied to the early Little Theatres by cynical husbands. There was some justification for this half-amused, half-contemptuous dismissal of amateur dramatics from consideration by the hundred-percent citizen of Main Street, since the founding of the pioneer theatres was sparked almost entirely by the dowagers and the club matrons. To the average husband it was just one more woman's club or some such fiddle-faddle with a trick name; it was no place for a self-respecting man to be seen except for a few moments late at night, when he stopped by after the poker game to drive his wife home from rehearsal. When he did not amiably dismiss the whole thing as a lot of foolishness, he was suspicious of its potentialities for irregular behavior.

Puritanism was still respectable, and far from dead. Very much alive, too, was the frontier tradition which pictured all actresses as (to use the delightful Victorian euphemism) no better than they should be, and all actors either as hyperthyroid Lotharios or effeminates with unmentionable tendencies.

The fact that the people with whom his wife was associating were amateurs and therefore not under the compulsion of hunger made it all the worse. Obviously something shady was afoot, and the worst elements in the city were seizing the opportunity for unbridled license under the protective cloak of culture.

When not obsessed by such fears as these, the husband resented the disturbance of his domestic routine and became embittered by repeated calls on his pocketbook. The picture of Mr. Ritter in The Torchbearers is a very fair representation of the typical theatre-widower of that day, and to thousands of other husbands their wives' Little Theatre associates looked exactly like Mrs. Pampanelli and her troupe.

With the establishment of more secure economic foundations and the building of their own auditoriums the early community theatres no longer had to rehearse in living rooms and perform in rented halls. Their new stages were not always very spacious, the lighting was sometimes less than adequate, but the equipment usually included a mortgage of some size. Here was something the businessmen could understand and be interested in. A few of them were prevailed upon to serve on the boards of trustees; perhaps their sporting instincts were aroused and they were intrigued with the idea of experimenting with new methods of amortization. It is a calumny to accuse the American businessman of feeling no interest in any but successful and prosperous civic enterprises, because many of them are actually stimulated by the prospect of a little money-raising and scientific budgeting.

With these attractive new names on the board indicative of security and stability in their management, the amateurs gained stature in the eyes of the general citizenry. It was obvious that the theatres were now being conducted along businesslike lines, and the department stores opened credit accounts with great alacrity.

Then the trustees began to engage professional directors instead of hiring dramatic coaches. Alexander Dean (Little Theatre Organization and Management) and Oliver Hinsdell (Making The Little Theatre Pay) wrote books which gave more than a rough outline of the kind of man who should be engaged. The new directors seemed to be quite regular fellows; some of them even had a head for business of an elementary sort, and they made the suggestion that budgets should be set up and reserve funds established to take care of an expanded program.

Many influences combined to change the attitude of the average citizen from his original mixture of condescension and distrust to one of at least impersonal pride in his city's theatre group. There was publicity value for Dallas, for instance, in the winning of a national drama tournament three years in succession. In quite a number of cities, the Chambers of Commerce publicized the community theatre as an inducement to new residents and even furnished active backing and support. The Little Theatre was now reputable and the era of "The Torchbearers" was ended. Today George Kelly's lampoon is no more than a period piece.

Despite the undeniable growth of public esteem for the theatre in principle, there are still a great number of misapprehensions regarding the exact status of the amateur who in the last analysis makes the theatre possible.

Granville Barker, in *The Exemplary Theatre*, insists that "there is no reason why a man should not be a first-class actor and give equally serious attention to other work." The converse is equally tenable. There is no reason why a man should not be a first-class lawyer, doctor, engineer, or automobile salesman and give equally serious attention to acting. An important law firm could afford to give active encouragement to its junior partner's acting ambitions or a department store give more than merely tacit consent to the community theatre activities of its staff members.

In such cases the indulgence of an avocation has a special value and serves as added technical education. For my production of *The Last Mile* several years ago the district attorney not only lent his whole arsenal of confiscated weapons and numbered exhibits, but asked me to cast three of his assistants in appropriate roles. As a talented and experienced actor himself, he appreciated the value to young lawyers of a disciplined memory and the ability to control an audience.

In another city the largest department store actively encourages its salespeople to join and work for the community playhouse and, in addition, offers free classes in Speech and Dance after business hours. The executives of the firm are frank to admit they realize considerable return on this investment in the increased poise and alertness of their workers and the improved morale which proceeds from a fellowship of interest in other than routine work.

These recognitions of the positive commercial value of a theatrical avocation are utterly commendable and of tremendous value to any community group. A director would be carrying idealism too far if he inquired too closely into the motives of every prospective participant. It is sufficient for him that they are willing and able. They furnish the willingness and the director must determine the ability.

The purely recreational aspect of any avocation is universally recognized and accepted, but as far as the theatre is concerned this recognition is for passive rather than active participation. Attendance at the play is no longer under puritanical taboo and the citizens who stay away do so not on principle, but because they definitely prefer other forms of entertainment or find them more economical than the drama.

The majority of the people who want actively to participate rarely give any thought to their psychological motives. They have not analyzed themselves and diagnosed a case of exhibitionism, inferiority, or inhibition. They just want to act. Perhaps they are looking for fun, or an opportunity to meet new people and make new friendships, or just something to do. They are very little concerned with the art, but they expect to be instructed in the craft of their new avocation. It is the director's problem to decide whether they are to be pieces on his chessboard, clay for his fashioning, or interesting individual human beings to be inspired to their highest potentialities.

They are very little concerned with the art

For the purposes of an avocation with therapeutic overtones it is sufficient that the theatre will afford opportunities for training in leadership; that it will improve co-ordination and emotional control; that it will teach the value of co-operation and the danger of indifference. It will stress concentration and precision, a sense of order and punctuality. This is a formidable list of benefits to be derived from a single prescription.

Any director has seen this medicine used in a hundred cases and will be prepared to vouch for its efficacy. But his job is to produce plays, not to perform as psychiatrist and father-confessor. His main interest is to cast and rehearse the plays so that the finished production will do everybody credit, including the author. The other tasks are incidental, but none the less inescapable.

There will be occasions when some player will, with utter simplicity and honesty, confess that the role he is rehearsing is beyond him. He is not "getting it," and he offers the director a chance to replace him before it is too late. There will be times when an actress has no thought of giving up her part, but is confused by some piece of business, some reading of a line that baffles her. She has tried, is willing to go on trying, but it only seems to get worse. She throws herself on the director's mercy.

I hope that my colleagues will agree that such incidents, distressing as they are to the victims, should cause great joy to the director. He will have discovered a sensitive soul with a capacity for self-analysis, with a feeling of responsibility. It is on such occasions that the director is grateful for the opportunity of saying and doing the right thing. It is a crossroads for the player and a challenge to his leader.

It is far more rewarding to have to persuade a conscientious player to hang on to his part or to help a struggling young actress to overcome a "block" than to contend with the other types, the exhibitionist insensitive to correction and criticism or the feather-brained fashion plate with her mind on her wardrobe.

These impervious individuals are the genuine misfits in the theatre because they let the theatre do nothing for them. They give not, neither do they take; they are completely self-sufficient and self-complacent, they give the play no assistance and they derive no benefit from their experience. It is the sensitive ones, unsure of their ability to do justice to the play, but willing to sacrifice themselves for it, who are the raw material of which fine actors are made.

CHAPTER THIRTEEN

How Good Is a Good Amateur?

THE AVERAGE COMMUNITY PLAYER DOES NOT CONSCIOUSLY OFFER less than his best. The trouble is that few people, often not even his directors, ever tell him how much better he could be. Mere carping criticism, sarcasm, and nagging will not help, and the actor himself must be receptive to suggestions for the improvement of his performance. He must have, in St. Augustine's words, "The modesty of a soul confessing its defects."

The players who take counsel with the director to try to discover in what way they can improve, or even offer to resign the part in favor of someone who is better equipped will do finer work each year; no standard will be too high for them to aim at. To them the theatre is not merely a hobby; it is an avocation and a serious one.

It is the hobbyist who is the misfit and who gives the title of amateur its low estate. He loves himself more than he loves his work and when cornered he falls back on the old excuse— "But I'm only an amateur, after all!"

Well, the Harvard-Yale game (or Yale-Harvard, as preferred) is played by "amateurs," but if anyone fumbles the ball, the offender does not turn to the booing crowd and cry, "Let me down lightly, boys, I'm only an amateur." Nor do the glee

There are good and bad in each

clubs from those schools deprecate the possible adverse comments of the metropolitan music critics by that same plaintive wail.

The best community production of any play cannot stand comparison with the best professional production of the same work. Does that prove anything? There are a great many professional productions, even on Broadway, that are below first class standard just as there are, unfortunately, many community presentations that are even more regrettable. That proves even less.

The point is that "professional" and "amateur" need not represent different grades of competence. Leaving economic considerations on one side, they are merely categories and there are good and bad in each category. Beyond that I refuse to be drawn at this point.

how good CAN he be?

At the risk of being classed with the mourners who contend all good acting died with Bernhardt I want to say that there were many fine actors in the pioneering days of the community theatre whose performances I have not seen bettered. Viewed in perspective, in the light of today's fashionably restrained playing, some of these performances might not be so highly esteemed (I never saw Bernhardt). But some of these early Little Theatre productions included performances that were white-hot with intensity, the work of fanatics who had the scornful laughter of Main Street in their ears and who had to be superlatively good and desperately in earnest in order to justify themselves.

Today the all-round level of competence is higher and many more people are able and willing to fill the roles. But it is a dead level of competence that they maintain and no more than that.

It is not difficult to assign some possible reasons. The war years doubled and trebled the size of the audiences without, unfortunately, increasing their discrimination. At the same time the acting companies were depleted, with most of the best young players in uniform and the middle-aged ones too occupied or anxious to be able to stand the grind of rehearsals. The few people who were available cannot be blamed if their talents did not measure up to those of their predecessors, but they should be criticized for taking things easy, regarding themselves as indispensable or mistaking the easy laughter of a wartime audience for critical acclaim.

In justice to those who gave of their best we have to remember that a feeling of impermanence and instability began to permeate our lives as far back as ten years ago. To some people the opportunity to rehearse and play a role was a temporary release from ever-present dread or anxiety. With the actual outbreak of war few people were capable of a whole-souled concentration on a make-believe which seemed trivial and not a little shameful against the background of world tragedy. It is not an implied criticism of the sensitivities of those who did participate to say that many of the finest community players simply could not bring themselves to act at all during the war. Some allowance must be made for these handicaps to production during the past six years, otherwise it would be impossible to avoid the conclusion that the nonprofessional standards were on the decline.

I cannot take such a pessimistic view, but I realize that it will be for me and my fellow-directors to raise the standards. We lay claim to a superior theatre intelligence, to a wider knowledge of plays and players, and we therefore should be the best judges of the acting in our companies. We must be satisfied with nothing less than the best.

HOW GOOD *SHOULD* HE BE?

Perhaps that question has already been answered. He should be as good as his ideals, as good as his conscience and his director can make him. He must forget "amateur" and "professional" and strive for excellence of itself. He must realize his full potentialities, even if he has to stop now and then for a check-up, for self-analysis, or to commune with the director, confident of help and sympathy.

Christopher St. John, the biographer of Ellen Terry and editor of *Ellen Terry and Bernard Shaw; A Correspondence* speaks, in the latter book, of "the saintly humility which was one of Miss Terry's most precious qualities" and adds that "although reckoned by many a genius, with fifty years of stage experience behind her she still felt she had much to learn." To a lesser degree, perhaps, all great artists allow themselves some diffidence and are constantly seeking for perfection.

This self-analysis does not imply any loss of confidence in one's own powers. I have stressed the value to all players, amateur or professional, of the right kind of self-confidence, which has no relation whatever to self-complacency. It is possible for an actor to face an audience with courage and assurance and yet be less than satisfied with his performance. A good job can always be bettered.

How good is the amateur? On the average, much better than he was twenty-five years ago. Training, experience, added public respect for his avocation, — all have combined to produce a competent nonprofessional type.

How good can he be? As good as he will allow himself to be. Ellen Terry was still trying after fifty years on the stage.

How good should he be? There are limitations to talent and physical equipment, but none to honesty, sincerity, and truth.

CHAPTER FOURTEEN

The Temperamentals

PERSONALITY IS THE DISTINGUISHING QUALITY OF AN INDIVIDUAL, that which marks him from his fellows. It is a matter of degree, not an absolute quantity, since all human beings possess a personality of some kind. To say that a person lacks personality is an obvious contradiction in terms.

But what in the entertainment world—the theatre, the movies, the radio—is meant by personality is the quality which sets some people apart by reason of their ability to mesmerize their audience, to pour themselves out so lavishly that the beholder (or the listener) is literally constrained to reciprocate by attention and applause. By the degree to which this compelling force is exerted we estimate the power of the personality.

Since the use of personality implies this almost spendthrift outpouring of fervor it is not surprising that the moment for its use is not always well chosen. The very freedom from repression which marks the exceptional man or woman often leads them to undisciplined use of their powers. They forget the value of economy and selection; they over-act and they act out of season. These are "the temperamentals."

Temperamentalism may be described as the overflow from the reservoir of personality which the dam of artistic restraint and selection should be able to confine at the proper level. Unfortunately each individual receptacle is separate and distinct, and the height of the dams varies quite considerably, which means that some of them are prone to overflow with each emotional shower. This indicates a lack of restraint, of emotional control, and it is usually when the retaining walls are low and the reservoir is shallow that there is a continual, unchecked dribble of exhibitionism. The greater the restraint, the more evidence there is of power held in check by the confining walls.

In *The Flower in Drama* Stark Young describes talent as "a thing of the body. It goes back to the body, as music does to the ear-drum and the nerves of hearing; it gives an important continuity to the person, and makes it not only true but necessary that the greatest actors always in a sense act themselves."

There are some powerful personalities, people of great talent and charm, in the community theatre who do, in a sense, act themselves all the time. They are gifted with vigorous temperaments, and some of them incline to become temperamental. Under proper direction and sympathetic understanding, they can be controlled, and their energies harnessed to the uses of the theatre. They can be fitted into the pattern of the production and guided to the disciplined approach, but it will take a director of strong personality to achieve the desired results. He cannot himself be temperamental, he must exercise the quality of restraint and sympathy with such people to a much larger extent than he must with the placid, contained variety of amateur actors. Indeed, he may sometimes have to pour himself out in generous measure in order to animate some of the self-contained, repressed beings who do not know how to let themselves go. But with the temperamentals he will use the firm, restraining hand and the soothing voice.

The temperamentals may be divided into two general categories, of which the first embraces the various types of exhibitionist. This is the shallow variety, wasting what little power it has in "scenes" away from the stage or in demonstrations unrelated to the play. It makes up in egotism what it lacks in real personal power. People of this type are misfits who are positively destructive to theatre morale, and to inflate their egos by allowing them to play prominent parts will give them undeserved encouragement. Perhaps the best treatment for people who are so unjustifiably sure of themselves is a succession of small, unimportant parts until such time as the light begins to dawn and they realize their limitations.

The other type is the vigorous temperamental who has power, control, and magnetism on the stage and off. People of this kind are at once the director's joy and despair; joy because of the really magnificent heights to which they can sometimes rise, despair because of their tendency to spill over at unexpected moments.

The talented temperamentals give life to a production. They are the "stars" who have the range and variety necessary to sustain the long roles. They act as inspirers and pacemakers to the less experienced players and they frequently reward the director by superlative performances.

They are often quite severe critics of their own work and will, just as earnestly as the sincere young beginner, analyze their performances in search of improvement. Sometimes they are not too wise in the choice of the moment to do this. In the middle of rehearsal they decide to assume an attitude of helpful helplessness: "You *must* show me what to do. There *must* be a better way to read that line . . ."; or in affected despair: "I don't know what's the matter with me. I've never had this trouble with a part before"; or feeling slighted: "Why don't you spend some time giving *me* some new business?"

They are begging for encouragement, for reassurance. They do not need extravagant praise, nor do they demand it. They are actually quite sure of their ability eventually to realize the proper characterization, but they need an appreciative audience all the time, even though it be only an audience of one. A sympathetic director supplies that need, and he can gain more on such occasions by warmth and sympathy than by preoccupation with technical deficiencies. For the word of criticism there is a time and a place, but it is not at such moments when the actor is at the director's mercy, begging for encouraging confirmation, and in front of the other actors in whose eyes the star must be allowed to do no wrong.

Players of this game are conscious, sometimes perhaps too much so, of their roles as leaders. While they are apt to appear regally aloof, something akin to a realization of noblesse oblige usually saves them from actual arrogance or condescension. They are more usually happy in the character of Lady Bountiful than of Marie Antoinette, and when the patronizing manner does make its appearance no great harm is ever done; the younger players handle that situation by being extravagantly amused and the Royal Family really impress no one but themselves by their antics.

But royalty, even the stage variety, lays claim to some privileges. Like the Lowells and Cabots, the theatre oligarchy takes for granted its right to a clear channel to the highest authority. The temperamentals demand a very close relationship with the director which is apt to grow in intensity as rehearsals proceed. There may be nothing personal in this intercourse, and once the play has closed the director may see or hear nothing of his closest collaborators until another suitable part brings them around once more. But as rehearsals quicken in tempo a tremendous intimacy is likely to develop; the leading performers become almost loverlike in their jealousy, and their resentment of the time the director spends coaching the smaller rôles is sometimes very real.

This desire for a close communion between the director and his players has to be fostered. The necessity for a warm relationship between him and the principal players who carry the main emotional burden of the play is especially great. There has to be developed a sort of mutual ardor, a reciprocal outpouring of personality. It is a perpetual private performance for an audience of one.

The wear and tear on the director is quite likely to be considerable, for he may have to maintain these intimate, but quite professionally impersonal relationships with several mercurial beings at one time. Moreover he has to strike a judicious balance and avoid giving too much overt attention to any one of his vis-à-vis in these attachments. Any tactics which are too obvious will be construed as showing partiality and will be keenly resented by the others. Or, what is more loaded with dynamite, giving too much attention to anyone may arouse the indignation of the player concerned as tending to spotlight his imperfections. There are pitfalls all along the road.

One very effective actor, the first time we worked together, presented me with a totally different characterization at each of the first four or five rehearsals. After some judicious sleuthing I found out he was a rabid movie fan with sufficient leisure to be able to attend a matinee every day if he so desired. At the evening rehearsal he would faithfully reproduce the distinguishing characteristics of the star he had seen in the afternoon. This chameleon quality certainly lent variety to our sessions but his fellow-players didn't appreciate his versatility. It was difficult for them to make the rapid adjustment necessary to play in support of everyone from Noel Coward to Paul Muni by way of Jean Hersholt, Charles Boyer, and John Barrymore.

As soon as I discovered the cause of these wide fluctuations in style I removed him from temptation either by calling afternoon rehearsals or taking him out on the golf course until such time as the proper characterization was established. Actually he was a capable performer in his own personal style and had no need of imitative methods.

Another very lovable character who once played Hamlet for me took his assignment with becoming seriousness. When not under the intoxicating influence of a leading role he was wont to dress very colorfully, but on beginning rehearsals he usually adopted some appropriate costume details to help his characterization. Starting to work on Hamlet he began by putting away all his more vivid neckgear and appearing every evening with a tie of solid black. A few days later, as his characterization grew in intensity, he showed up wearing a dark blue suit, a week later he changed to an oxford grey, and finally settled down to a black affair which he wore day in, day out, until the dress rehearsal. At that time, without transitional shock, he stepped into the garb of the sweet prince, fully conditioned to somber and melancholy hues.

I retained my composure pretty well during this period of what the electrician called "Hamlet's slow dim-out"; it would have been cruel to laugh or even to permit a smile in public, and it would have been fatal to allow the rest of the cast to offer any comment.

The final example of artistic integrity came about a week before the opening, when Hamlet traded in his almost new dark green sedan for a similar model—painted black. The cast only recovered in time for the first night, but as their fellow-player was universally popular and a good companion at rehearsals he never knew how near they came to slaying the publicity man, who wanted to write a feature story on the event.

Hamlet gave a good account of himself in performance, the public was appreciative and we ran an extra week, so what did it matter if a conscientious actor did take himself a little too seriously?

CHAPTER FIFTEEN

The Audience and the Community

∿∿

THE TICKET BUYER IS THE FORGOTTEN MAN OF THE THEATRE, often completely overlooked in the calculations of the policy makers. An audience is regarded as a necessary evil and, as such, is tolerated and given a modicum of consideration, since by its presence it makes possible the paying of the bills and the taking of curtain calls. That both money and applause are essential is recognized by everyone around the theatre.

But a proper recognition of the audience as an actual instrument in the making of policy is something else again. Provided that the crowds keep coming, raise no violent protest, and applaud with the average amount of warmth, the community theatres are apt to accept public support with the utmost complacency and go on doing the plays they always have done. In consequence their productions tend to be imitative and standardized, rarely creative, original, or courageous in furnishing a lead to audience taste and discrimination. The people "out front" are taken for granted, and taken at a very low valuation at that.

The play selectors will, of course, deny this. "We do take our subscribers into our confidence," they will say. "We try to find out what they want, and then arrange our schedule accordingly. We have conducted audience polls every season, for years."

This is quite true, as far as it goes. There are very few groups who do not make this gesture to their audiences, and almost every director has given careful study to the findings of these polls. What do they prove, beyond the immutable fact that the majority vote is always for "comedies"? If the questionnaire should list actual titles so that the voters could indicate their preference for seven or eight out of a total of twenty or more, the preponderance of the selections will always be plays currently successful on Broadway, or plays which have recently closed but are now being highly publicized by Hollywood because of the forthcoming release of a picture by the same name. Public taste in entertainment, as in many other matters, is highly sensitive to propaganda, and we have to accept the fact that practically the only sources of information for the average theatregoer are the syndicated column, the gossip paragraph, and the photograph with the flattering caption. This is just as true of the Manhattan resident as of the subscriber to the Middletown Playhouse.

A very vivid illustration of the carrying power of the press agent's trumpet was our experience at Memphis one year. The audience at the last play of the season was provided with a list of some twenty-five plays from which they were asked to select eight as their choice for the following season. The names of the authors were not shown. The first title printed on the list was *My Heart's In The Highlands.* It topped the poll, which was not surprising because every candidate for public office knows that the leading name on the ticket starts with an undue advantage over those which follow.

The title of the play is definitely arresting, suggestive of romance, of love in the open spaces. It is a box-office name, but I felt sure that very few of the voters knew of the author of the play. Since many of the subscribers signed their names to their selections I was able to do a little sampling on my own account and discovered, as I had suspected, that the appeal of the title was the only reason for about ninety percent of these votes. When I mentioned that the author was William Saroyan, they were not so sure they had chosen wisely, and when I outlined the plot at their request there was a further diminution of enthusiasm. Although we were genuinely anxious to do the play and so test its audience appeal in the only practical way, I recall some difficulty about obtaining the rights of production and the good people of Memphis were therefore spared considerable disillusionment. They were also, incidentally, deprived of the chance of seeing what George Jean Nathan has called "as bonny, imaginative, and utterly fascinating a sentimental lark as came in a long spell." But some of them, at least, would have had some trouble in reconciling the matter of the play with the preconceived notions prompted by the title.

In the same poll, hidden away in the center of the list, was *The Little Foxes*, at that time running strongly on Broadway. It had not yet been purchased by Hollywood and the character of Regina was therefore not even a gleam in Miss Bette Davis' eye. Tallulah Bankhead was remembered by the greater public, if at all, as just another stage actress who had not made the grade in Hollywood. To knowing New Yorkers she was an established star playing the finest role of her career, but it was only after our poll had been in progress three or four days that the front pages of every newspaper in the country carried some story or other which gave her considerable prominence. As it was intended to do, the paragraph made no secret of the fact that she was rather prominently associated with *The Little Foxes*.

Up to that time very few votes had been cast for that play, but the evening following the appearance of the news story at least 75 percent of the Memphis audience marked *The Little Foxes* on their lists. The sound of the press agent's trumpet carries a long way.

These samplings of public preference prove very little beyond the fact that the overall result of a national poll on any question—international policy, birth control, the most popular movie star, or the most acceptable program of plays—will be fairly accurately reflected by the opinion of any one local group. Sectional prejudices or recognized regional tendencies will account for some minor variations, but within a few percentage points the national preference may usually be discovered by taking any city as a sample. Thus, an audience poll in Memphis would show just about the same evidence of audience taste as one taken the same week in Minneapolis. Both cities are subjected to the same propaganda barrage, for the gossip columns are ubiquitous. The law of averages has yet to be disproved, and although every city likes to proclaim its individuality insofar as taste in entertainment is concerned, the fact remains that as Broadway goes, so goes the nation—a few months later.

The choice, then, for the policy makers is whether they want to supply the average audience or the distinctive one. Do they plan a theatre which is just like every other, or do they want one so different—by reason of careful nurture—that it will be a landmark, and set a standard for others to emulate?

The swollen audiences of the past few war years have been very welcome to all treasurers and guarantors. Many a mortgage has been burned and many an overdraft liquidated. Quite a few reserve funds have been created to take care of expansion of one kind or another.

The size of these new subscription lists and the noise of the applause are positively dangerous. Some few far-sighted makers of policy are asking themselves whether they really want to keep on playing each production two and even three weeks, although the audiences continue to register approval.

The actors are overworked, they say, their performances tend to grow casual, and preparation of the next production is either delayed or rushed. Even with the funds in hand it will not be possible to build the necessary additional facilities for rehearsals within the next few years. "Can we keep up the pace?" they are asking. "Will the audiences start to fall off just about the time these extra facilities are available—and will the ones who are left be the type of subscriber we want? Will the discriminating have been driven away by the undistinguished plays we have had to do (we polled our audience, you know), and will the residue be merely distraction-seekers?" The last of these prospects is the most appalling, for the theatre whose subscription list has dwindled to its prewar size but contains only "the unskillful" would be in the position of having to start all over again with the task of building an audience.

This would be a disheartening, backbreaking task, because audience taste has to be created and trained, patiently and painstakingly, and the job is not done in any one season. The difference between the civic theatre and Broadway, between the community theatre of distinction and the "average" one is just this matter of a trained, discriminating clientele. Of necessity its personnel changes slightly every year, but the turnover among its supporters should be very small if the job of creating an audience—and not merely selling tickets—is being well done.

I am not advocating an "art theatre" program, an undiluted fare of indigestible foreign translations and classics, in the narrow sense. A program of that type belongs to a college theatre which is interested in exposing its students to the genuine world drama and to plays which are educational if not always entertaining. A drama school might be excused for regarding its audience as a necessary evil.

The goal for the community policy makers should be a diversified repertory with gradually rising standards both of material and performance. There should always be under consideration a play which cannot be done well enough this year but which must be done the next. And next year should mean the following season, not the tomorrow which never comes.

The average audience member does not know what he wants, he only thinks he does, but he should not be despised or ignored on that account. There must be neither pity nor contempt in the attitude of the theatre towards its supporters, but there has to be a feeling of grave responsibility. The theatres which have maintained an unbroken record of operation for twenty and twenty-five years are the ones which have entertained this responsibility and kept raising their standards of repertory and production. These groups refused to compromise, they paid not too much attention to polls and audience surveys and if the present time does find some of them filling their houses by playing the less distinguished type of Broadway farce-comedy, their record is sufficient assurance of their ability to lead their audiences rather than to be led.

I see no reason for the general assumption that membership must of necessity fall within a few years to little higher than the prewar level, or that, on the other hand, the community theatres must throw overboard their standards and play down to these new and admittedly less discriminating audiences. For this reason I have never been able to share the enthusiasm of some colleagues for the closed membership policy which they advocate as the only solution of the membership problem. Their well-reasoned attitude is that it is the casual ticket buyer who demands, and makes necessary, the production of spurious and trivial plays, and that only regular attendance at all productions over a period, not of one season merely but of a number of years, will equip any member of a theatre audience with the necessary keenness of perception and perfection of taste.

If it were possible to garner a subscription list consisting of theatre devotees with a life expectancy of at least ten years and be assured that in addition to the mere promise of survival they would also be one hundred percent free from all sickness, domestic tribulations, or financial reverses, it is feasible that a watertight little coterie of theatregoers might be able to reach incredible heights of taste and appreciation. But such a desideratum is unattainable on the face of it; all available statistics go to prove that many factors combine to make a seasonal turnover inevitable even when there is a high level of satisfaction with the program. Even scientifically managed concert series such as The Civic Music Association, which offer highly desirable musical attractions of the first rank sometimes experience a turnover in their subscription lists of as high as sixty percent. Death, removal, economic disturbance, fluctuations in taste, all take their toll; there is no such thing as a stable audience, or even a ninety percent constant body of playgoers.

Another fallacy in the argument for the exclusive type of membership lies in the assumption that the coterie will consist entirely of persons who are either impeccable in their dramatic taste or who are capable of being molded closer to the desire of the selectors of the repertory. This is mere wishful thinking. There is no guarantee that the purchaser of a season ticket may not be that undesirable individual the Philistine, the devotee of bedroom farce, or even the thin-skinned puritan of deplorably Comstockian views. Either such irreconcilable elements in the audience would have to be endured for several years or else encouraged to resign out of hand. In the latter case the problem would be to discover whether the next names on the waiting list might not be those of similarly inharmonious citizens. The only safe way to select the ideal audience would be by a questionnaire or some other equally objectionable form of inquisition. The possibilities of such a procedure are limitless, and quite terrifying.

It would seem to be more sporting to place no restrictions on admission, but to allow prospective new members to sample the wares by allowing them to make their own choice of individual plays before accepting their subscriptions for a whole season. It might be the policy of wisdom to prepare some new subscribers in this way to take the place of the ones who will drop out of the list each year by reason of death, debt, or dissatisfaction.

A policy which invites a subscription list to produce an income large enough to remove financial worry and then permits nonsubscribers to purchase single admissions is in general practice today. Admittedly it is a compromise but a realistic one. The repertory for the season is selected with the subscribers in mind; the casual visitor (who, it is hoped, is also the prospective subscriber) incurs some slight risk of surprise or disappointment, since he may have been misled by the play's title. The regular subscribers run almost the same risk, but they do not expect complete satisfaction from every play. In general they are reasonable and view the entire season in proper perspective before deciding whether or not to renew their subscriptions. Moreover, as subscriber-members they feel something of proprietorship and the right to complain about a play they do not like, but they are unwilling to allow the same privilege to the casual visitor. They will defend the policy, the play selection, and the production standards of their theatre against the criticism of the outsider. It is right and proper for them to feel possessive.

But, by being prepared to admit anyone who presents himself at the box office with the price of admission the theatre preserves the genuine spirit of community participation. Only if there are no restrictions on admission is it logical and equitable for the group to function in the name of a community or civic theatre and enjoy all the privileges and perquisites appertaining thereto such as discounts, free publicity, and the loan of furniture.

In justice to some of the most eloquent spokesmen for the closed membership school of thought it must be admitted that they do not speak in terms of a community theatre in the accepted sense. They are vitally interested in a better national theatre, with higher standards all around, and their plan has met with success in several cities where the theatre does not operate on avowedly "community" lines.

Unfortunately this theory finds favor with a number of other groups at present agitated by the problem of large subscription lists, consequent long runs, and limitations of space. These groups have a responsibility to their communities and they can hope to retain their democratic appeal and their civic esteem only by encouraging the widest possible support. I believe that any attempt to close their membership would bring about an unfavorable reaction.

The method adopted to derive income for the theatre is

closely bound up with the problem of building an audience. The closed membership plan has the merit of allowing the group to concentrate upon a reasonably unified body of people. With the subscription-plus-box-office plan the audience personnel will change more frequently but the plays are constantly reaching and attracting a larger group of the citizens. There is no absolute saturation point.

I know of no prominent group which operates without a subscription policy in some form or other except the Palo Alto Community Theatre where Ralph Emerson Welles has so impressed the city government with the value of the theatre's work that his organization receives an annual subsidy of considerable size.

Norris Houghton, author of *Advance From Broadway*, says, "The first question that arises in the mind of a visitor is to what extent a city-owned and operated theatre is affected by political interference or censorship. Mr. Welles is able to say there is none; and he claims that the theatre's democratic policy is responsible."

Despite the comfortable feeling of financial security and the sincerity of Mr. Welles' assurances, most theatre groups would, I feel, prefer complete independence even at the cost of some financial headaches. They are willing to entertain responsibility to the community as a whole, but it must be their own interpretation of the measure of this obligation. This interpretation is usually that the community deserves the best that can reasonably be furnished in the way of dramatic entertainment.

Perfectionists may find this credo overcautious, a counsel of expediency, a compromise with ideals. To Norris Houghton, who in 1940 viewed the community scene through Broadway-tinted glasses, this very caution seems to imply satisfaction with mediocrity. He found the regional theatre paying no attention to social injustices, neglecting "the workers," charging such high prices that only a low percentage of any city's population could afford to partake of what was no more than a watered-down version of Broadway.

The years since his odyssey have only slightly altered the picture and rendered invalid only a few of his reflections. The audiences have increased in size, in some cases threefold, giving most theatres a potential far in excess of the most optimistic expectations of the original pioneers. The prices charged for admission have, in general, remained at 1940 levels, the increase in the total cost of a ticket being attributable to the entertainment tax paid without protest by a public hardened to such exactions. In comparison with the cost of other distractions, the price of a community theatre ticket in 1947 seems very reasonable.

His other comments still have some justification but Mr. Houghton perhaps may have misunderstood the functions and the responsibilities of the present-day community theatre. The art theatre of the '20's has outlived its usefulness. Twenty-five years ago it filled a desperate need and there are those of us who fought its early battles who believe that it fulfilled its purpose. It was not without definite influence on public taste, on production standards, and even on Broadway repertory. No matter who claims the credit for the undoubted improvement, a comparison between Burns Mantle's *Ten Best Plays* of 1940 and those of twenty years earlier will prove something.

Kenneth Macgowan, writing ten years or so before Norris Houghton, found the community theatre grown-up, leaving amateurism for professionalism. In *Footlights Across America* he says that "It is just possible, however, that we may find the finished product not only an art theatre or a repertory theatre or whatever we may care to label it, but also a theatre serving a bigger audience than it ever served before. A community theatre—at last and for perhaps the first time." He significantly ended this chapter by having the printer affix the signet of the Birmingham (England) Repertory Theatre which, under Sir Barry Jackson, has served its community for over thirty years with the highest possible standards of production.

Mr. Macgowan's prophecy is in process of fulfillment. The objective of most community theatres is to serve the citizens with a program of dramatic entertainment. The professional directors are charged with the duty of maintaining—and improving—the standards of direction, acting, and production, and it is only at those groups which are more interested in the number of active participants than in the quality of performance that criticism should be leveled.

Mr. Houghton penetrated the forest primeval and roamed the wide open spaces in search of something he had been told was at once exotic and native. He searched for a primitive art form and a "living newspaper" and of course found neither.

Instead he found something quite positive and vital—an agglomeration of producing organizations, each of them self-supporting, dependent neither upon subsidy (Palo Alto, of course, being a notable exception) nor upon the bounty of patronage, working out their own individual problems and free from the domination of any cult or fad.

Largely by the process of trial and error, most theatre groups have evolved a policy and a style in repertory and production that meet with the approval of their public. But the theatre's responsibility does not end here and audience commendation cannot be presumed to be unfailing. To say that theatre attendance becomes a habit is to ignore the fact that habits may be broken when a more exciting form of diversion comes along. The inner core of theatre fanatics are apt to credit the general theatre public with the same devotion they themselves possess. They take the audience for granted because they themselves could not live without the flesh-and-blood drama, good, bad, or indifferent in quality.

Even if the membership is at present larger each year than the one before, too great a turnover in the personnel of the subscribers should be interpreted as a danger signal. More people fail to renew their support through loss of interest than by death or removal, and although few of those who drop out are ever completely candid about their reasons for non-renewal, their privacy must be respected. There may be many other reasons for their withdrawal besides "I do not like the kind of plays . . . ," but in any case a poll of disgruntled ex-subscribers is not recommended.

In a previous chapter on Play Selection I suggested a judicious admixture of two apparently conflicting policies. The audience must be given what they want and also what they ought to want. Completely to ignore the first desideratum is to court financial disaster; to overlook the second is to shirk responsibility for the creation of an audience which will not only be distinctive itself but will support an organization of increasing excellence.

There is no sure formula beyond patience and a sort of stubborn adherence to ideals. Perhaps no American theatre will ever repeat the revolutionary work of Antoine or Stanislavsky. But the new audiences of today are a challenge, and the evolutionary process may be the way to meet it. If the directors of the American regional theatres have a sufficient breadth of vision to enable them to accept the challenge, to give their repertory some backbone, and their productions an individual "form and pressure," then their communities will have been well served and a new and more worthy theatre created on the foundations of the present one.

CHAPTER SIXTEEN

Looking Around

〜〜〜〜〜〜〜〜〜〜〜〜〜〜〜〜〜〜〜〜〜〜〜〜〜〜〜〜〜〜〜〜〜〜〜〜〜〜〜

TO VIEW THE NATIONAL PICTURE WITH ABSOLUTE DETACHMENT
is to be forced to the conclusion that most community theatre
groups are at the present time indulging in what may turn out
to be a fatal complacency. To keener observers than myself a
new order is in the making and the national theatre—for that
is the only way properly to describe this conglomeration of
separate, individual, and unregimented play-producing organizations—is literally at the crossroads. Most of these groups
seem quite unaware that they have arrived at a turning point
and that a decision is being forced upon them.

On the face of it the leading groups are in a stronger position
than ever before. In the foregoing chapters I have made frequent references to the growing subscription lists, to the long
runs of each play that these large audiences make necessary.
The people who fill these auditoriums are no longer merely the
friends of the players, the social climbers and the culture seek-
ers. The American nonprofessional theatre has come a long
way since Harold Markham, author of *The Amateur Theatrical Handbook*, could write, in 1927, that: "Amateurs, it can
thankfully be remembered, play to *amateur audiences*—to
people who have come to make the best of them, not coldly to
demand value for money. Our audiences are not 'hundred-
headed beasts' but our best friends."

The ticket buyer of today makes very little distinction between a professional and an amateur provided the play is one he wants to see, and provided the recommendation of his friends is sufficiently warm. Very few road companies now deem it necessary or even desirable to advertise that they are presenting a "New York cast," because audiences are more sophisticated than they were; they know, from reading their papers that the original New York cast is still playing on Broadway, has been playing there for three, four, or five years in fact, and cannot, therefore, be in two places at once. If highly publicized stars are not billed in the cast, a road company is just another competent group of players. And competence may as readily be found today at the local civic theatre in a residential section as at the "legit" house downtown.

Since the war New England and the contiguous states have been teeming with all kinds of summer theatre offerings. These companies have ranged all the way from completely professional, Equity-approved casts of Broadway caliber down to the most unripe examples of amateur improvisation. The scale of prices was almost uniform; it cost no more to see Helen Hayes than to watch the wife of a publisher, and a very healthy business was done by all. The audience seemed to ask no questions about the constitution of the company or the status of the players. They wanted a show, they paid to see it, and if it satisfied them, they came again the following week.

Even after due allowance is made for the fact that these have been years of easy spending, it is easy to draw the conclusion that, in the main, audiences no longer make great distinction between the professional and the nonprofessional, as such. They will, of course, always flock more readily to see Hayes, Cornell, or the Lunts than they will to a cast of unfamiliar players, but they will turn out to see *Life With Father* whether Howard Lindsay or his tenth, or one-hundredth, facsimile appears as the peppery parent. At the community production some local dramatic luminary may draw especially well, but provided the productions have a reputation for sustained competence the title of the play will be the principal attraction.

There are very few community theatres whose production standards, taken all around, will stand comparison with a professional company doing the same play. There are even fewer whose work is superior to that of the average road company. "So what?" reply hundreds of producing groups from the communities, "Who said we were professionals? We don't pretend to be anything more than amateurs!"

Yet these very people cannot be more highly flattered than to be told by some gushing member of the first-night audience that they were "even better than the Broadway company." A well-meant but uncritical compliment like that will run like wildfire backstage and make good conversation for weeks afterwards. But when it is hinted that Tallulah Bankhead or Fredric March need not lose any sleep on account of the local performance the comment is briskly resented, and the offended players take refuge in their amateur status. Being human, they want to be praised in terms of the professional but criticized in terms of the nonprofessional. In short they want to have their cake and eat it too.

The nonprofessional theatre has to decide, and decide quickly, what it prefers to do with its cake. It has to make up its mind which course to pursue if it is to serve its communities with the best possible kind of theatre, irrespective of the status of the participants. If the simon-pure amateur can do it satisfactorily, and maintain a sufficiently high standard, many people would prefer to have it so. Not only the governing bodies but some of the professional directors of prominence have taken a firm stand in favor of the "preservation of the amateur," but they are in a minority of the leaders of the city groups. While there must always be a place for the wholesome avocational approach to theatricals in the rural districts and for church and club groups in a community of any size, the larger theatres, by reason of their investment in plant and equipment, their budgets and their subscription lists, are sub-

"You were better than the Broadway company."

ject to comparison if not to competition with the best that is available to their fellow-citizens. And that best is usually "the road" which has lately regained much of its old vigor. There are now more companies playing one-week stands than at any time since the early days of motion pictures.

The work of the Federal Theatre, that "undertaking at best experimental and delicate but carried out with skill and circumspection" as the Beards have described it, has borne fruit, however belatedly, as a builder of new audiences. It also helped to dispel some of the superstitions regarding the status of the actor, and caused no little confusion among its detractors, particularly those in Congress. These critics deplored the "waste of federal funds" but they seemed to be uncertain whether their objection was to payments being made to amateurs who were capable of doing *real work* or to professionals who were so incompetent that they ought not to be encouraged in their evil ways. The public attended or stayed away without giving much thought to the status of the performers. The productions served to exhibit the possibilities of the spoken drama for the first time to thousands of people who, after the abandonment of the federal project, turned to the community theatres and the road companies for comparable entertainment.

The civic entrepreneur has now to be as commercial as the downtown theatre manager. Both have overhead charges to meet and a public to satisfy and it is no longer a cogent argument that the nonprofessional company, whatever its standards of performance, has its own special public because its repertory is different, because the public can see plays in the little theatre that the professional producer would find unprofitable. Today the greatest ambition of most play selectors is to be able to perform the latest Broadway success before the road company brings it to town, an ambition rarely realized because of the restrictive efforts of the holders of the copyrights. These gentlemen pay the civic theatres the compliment of regarding them as serious competitors, which bears out the contention that whenever a well-established local group has built itself a sufficiently large audience it is regarded with respect by the so-called commercial theatre. Whether the group calls itself amateur or nonprofessional, or Civic, Little, or Community Theatre makes no difference; it is the possession of an audience for its productions which gives it importance.

After the drastic readjustments of the depression years, some few theatres achieved a genuinely professional outlook and had reorganized to meet the new conditions. Others were still pondering the advisability of enlarging the scope of their operations when the initiation of the defense program depleted their manpower and caused the abandonment of many ambitious schemes. The actual outbreak of war caused even further setbacks, the compulsion of the draft removing practically all the younger and more adventurous spirits from theatrical activity. In some localities the forces of reaction gathered strength and objected successfully not only to a more professionalized theatre but to any theatre at all. Incredible as it may seem now, there were, in 1942, many prominent and influential theatre patrons who went on record as believing it was morally wrong either to participate in or to attend the amateur theatre in wartime.

For one or another reason several groups suspended operations completely soon after Pearl Harbor. It was ironical that in the state of Texas, an armed camp with a wartime population of several million young men, thousands of them ardent and well-trained players and technicians, its three principal community groups were allowed to falter and die. The San Antonio Little Theatre, the Houston Community Players, and the Little Theatre of Dallas, all closed their doors within a few months of each other.

Not only in Texas are the young men and women back again from war service and, with the impatient vigor of youth, demanding a more adventurous approach. They are grateful to the people who kept some kind of theatre alive during the war years and they are quite bitterly critical of those who allowed it to die here and there. The adventurous spirits are already at

work on the rebuilding and the re-fashioning, in some cases
starting experimental groups of their own, in others exerting
pressure to obtain better standards, higher skills, and greater
competence in the existing groups.

The question of competence, and that does not mean mere
adequacy, is the crux of the matter. This whole argument of
"amateur or professional" revolves around the question whether
the nonprofessional can attain proper skill and competence in
the brief amount of time he has available to pursue a theatre
avocation.

The present long runs in community plays are exhausting to
a conscientious player who may raise no objection to four or
more weeks of strenuous rehearsal because these evenings do
include some intervals of relaxation and an occasional night
off. But the continuous playing of a role, with the concentration which this demands, is depleting to men and women even
if they do not have to be up betimes the following morning to
go about their regular business. Many community directors are
finding increasing reluctance among their better players to accept attractive roles because of the heavy demands of the
present schedules. Even if these valuable players are willing to
appear they are now limiting their contribution to one part in
a season, which means that the less competent players are
called upon. The audience is therefore deprived of the opportunity of seeing the best possible performance and the player
does not perform as often as he should if he is to maintain his
technique.

The problem of how to offer the public the best possible
production has never been more pressing. Scenically there is
little more that can be done within the limits of modern acceptance of stage illusion. Hollywood can surpass in realism
even the most lavish of Broadway settings. Any improvement
can, and must come, in the acting, in the presentation of ideas
and the interpretation of character. The acquisition of the
necessary skill to achieve this is a specialized and a full-time
occupation. The playing of one, or at the most, two parts in a

season is quite insufficient to keep an actor in playing condition, and it certainly limits his development. The chances are that he is a "type" to his director and will play the same kind of role again next season—and the next.

True, the Broadway professional often suffers long periods of idleness between shows but, in theory at least, he keeps in condition by exercise and study, and by occasional radio appearances. It is his professional duty and intelligent self-interest to maintain his technical equipment. The amateur has no such necessity; he has to plunge again into his vocation and perhaps work overtime for weeks in order to rid his desk of the accumulation of work occasioned by six weeks of memorizing, rehearsing, and performing in the play.

The proponents of the new national theatre point out that almost every department of the community theatre in any sizeable city is now professionalized. The director, the business manager, the technician-designer, and sometimes also a wardrobe mistress and a property man, are full-time workers on a salary. Only in the all-important department of acting is it assumed that the work is not sufficiently difficult to need adequate training and continuous, whole-time attention.

No revolution is proposed in order to establish this new order in the national theatre. The professional approach, the building of an acting company whose full time and energies are devoted to the perfection of their craft can best be achieved by the evolutionary process. It might start by the encouragement of some promising young community players, offering them some inducement to remain in their home city in return for a small weekly salary, guaranteed for the season. This last summer I received a request to recommend some young drama graduates for a community theatre which operates nine months a year and pays the members of its company small but regular salaries. Admittedly thirty-five dollars a week does not sound exciting to young actors whose friends may be currently making three times that amount on Broadway. But a Broadway production may run no more than four weeks and the next engagement be months, even years away, while the community theatre in question was offering its pittance for a guaranteed forty weeks of the theatrical year. At the end of that time, with a season of hard work, study, and the playing of a variety of roles to his credit, the young player would stand a better chance of conquering Broadway than with nothing to show but a few press clippings of his college and amateur appearances.

Moreover as his skill increased he would be more valuable to the local group if he wished to stay with them. From the community's point of view he should be encouraged to. The local theatre need not be regarded as a trade school, giving a few young actors each year just sufficient encouragement to leave at the end of the first season for New York, there to join the waiting lines outside the producers' offices. The proper conception of the new national theatre is that the regional company shall be an end and not merely the means.

Broadway and Hollywood will continue to exercise a powerful attraction, but every year more and more drama students grow to realize that these markets are hopelessly overcrowded and that their chances of even a small part in New York, followed by the offer of a Hollywood contract, are almost infinitesimal. The realistic attitude of such students is prompted by a desire to capitalize on their youth, to exploit their enthusiasm, to work at their vocation while they are still eligible for juvenile roles, and they feel that their own communities should manage to provide the necessary opportunities.

A theatre proposing to assemble a full-time company would very well begin by offering regular employment to two or three of these talented and well-trained players. Their agreement would call for their undivided attention to be given to the theatre. Gradually a few more could be added to give strength and variety to the resident company, but the professionalizing process need not mean that the amateur would become extinct. The change-over would be effected by constitutional methods extending over a number of years. It is not possible to foresee the time when the talented nonprofessional (i.e., the actor by avocation) would not, in individual cases, be invaluable in many productions. The older character parts, for instance, could not be played always to the satisfaction of the audience by the young professionals, however effective they might be on occasion. Gradually it might be economically possible to engage a few mature professionals from the outside, but for many years the community would need the services of the experienced middle-aged amateurs who are as a rule its most effective performers.

It is in the juvenile and the younger leading roles that the community companies must have the services of players who are not only talented, well-trained, and versatile, but who have the time to devote themselves to constant improvement and the opportunity, through regular full-time employment in their profession, to attain variety, power, and stage maturity. There would still be opportunity for the talented young people of the city who wished to join an apprentice group or workshop attached to the theatre in which they could learn by observation, study, and some practical experience.

The choice, then, should be fairly clear. There will always be a place for the amateur in the theatre as well as in the other arts. There will always be a place for the amateur producing organization, providing an outlet for self-expression and either devoted to experimentation in new forms or pursuing a quietly conventional course. Both of these two subdivisions of the frankly nonprofessional theatre would rely greatly upon the tolerance of the audience, the first making an appeal to a small, select group of playgoers who would be intrigued by the unusual, the second attracting a somewhat larger body of supporters who want anything but the unusual. In each case the amateur spirit would be predominant and the audiences would expect just so much, and no more.

But the new national theatre which the larger, more discriminating audience deserves and will eventually insist upon, will be controlled and staffed, and its performances executed, by specialists who will be community players because they have chosen to be, and who will still also be *amateurs* because, in the almost forgotten meaning of that word "they practice their art for the love of it."

A Contract for the Director *

Here is what seems to be a simple, direct, comprehensive contract; fair to both parties, and a model of its kind.

STATE OF . . . .

COUNTY OF . . . .

THIS AGREEMENT made and entered into this . . . . . day of . . . . . ., by and between the . . . ., Party of the First Part, and . . . ., Party of the Second Part,

WITNESSETH:

(1) Party of the First Part appoints the Party of the Second Part Director of the . . . . for the season . . . ., that is to say, September 15, ..., to June 15 . . . ., and the Party of the Second Part hereby accepts the aforesaid appointment on the terms and conditions hereinafter set forth, which are hereby agreed to.

(2) That in consideration of the services to be rendered by the Party of the Second Part as Director, the Party of the First Part agrees to pay the Party of the Second Part the sum of . . . . . . dollars in nine equal installments on or before the 15th day of each month of said term, commencing October 15, ..., and ending June 15 . . . .

(3) Party of the Second Part agrees to present seven productions of four performances each during said season, offering as many "repeats" and out-of-town performances

* From *Curtains Going Up* by Albert McCleery and Carl Glick. Pitman Publishing Corporation.

of said productions as to the President and/or Executive Committee of the .... in agreement with the said Director, may seem advisable.

(4) Party of the Second Part agrees to present each of the aforesaid seven productions according to the following schedule and within the times therein provided:

First—Between October 6 and October 23.

Second—Between November 10 and November 27.

Third—Between December 8 and December 25.

Fourth—Between January 20 and January 29.

Fifth—Between February 17 and March 2.

Sixth—Between April 21 and April 30.

Seventh—Between May 5 and May 15.

(5) Party of the Second Part agrees to keep all activities and expenditures, under his direction, within the limits of the budget as adopted by the Executive Committee and/or the Board of Governors, and the Party of the Second Part agrees to make no expenditures in excess of that provided by the aforesaid budget without the written approval of the Executive Committee or its duly constituted representative.

(6) Party of the First Part, subject to the aforesaid provisions and restrictions, hereby grants to the Party of the Second Part exclusive authority with reference to (a) choice of cast, (b) creation of productions within budgetary limits, and (c) selection of plays except that as to this item the said Director is to submit for the approval of the Board a list of not less than ten plays from which the productions for the year are to be chosen by agreement between said Director and the Board of Directors, such lists to be submitted not later than September 15 ....

(7) It is agreed that the Costume, Property and Stage

Staff Committee and their respective chairmen be selected by the Director, with the approval of the President.

(8) Party of the Second Part agrees to co-operate with and foster the activities of the .... and to do the utmost to advance the interest of the Party of the First Part.

(9) In addition to the compensation herewithin provided for, it is understood and agreed that the Party of the Second Part shall share in any income received by the Party of the First Part over and above the amount of the annual budget fixed by the Board of Directors for the ...... season in the following proportions: ......% of such overplus to the amount of ...... dollars; ......% of any excess over that; any amount due hereunder to be ascertained at the close of the season on June 15, ..., and any amount then found to be due to be then payable.

IN WITNESS whereof the ...., by its President and its Secretary, has caused its name to be hereunto subscribed and its seal to be hereunto affixed, and the said .... has hereunto set his hand and seal, both in triplicate, the date and the year first above written.

List of Plays Produced by

THE DALLAS LITTLE THEATRE 1920–1943

1920–1921

1. A Scrap of Paper: Victorien Sardou, adapted by J. Palgrave Simpson.
2. Between the Soup and the Savory:[1] Gertrude Jennings.
3. The Magistrate: Arthur Wing Pinero.
4. Green Stockings: A. E. W. Mason.
5. Nothing but the Truth: James Montgomery.
6. Beyond the Horizon: Eugene O'Neill.
7. The Rivals: R. B. Sheridan.
8. A Pair of Sixes: Edward Peple.

1921–1922

1. The Importance of Being Earnest: Oscar Wilde.
2. A Rose of Plymouth Town: B. M. Dix and E. G. Sutherland.
3. The Truth: Clyde Fitch.
4. { Wurzel-Flummery: A. A. Milne.
   { The Showing-up of Blanco Posnet: Bernard Shaw.
5. Mrs. Bumpstead-Leigh: Harry J. Smith.
6. Billeted: F. Tennyson Jesse and H. M. Harwood.
7. { Circumstantial Evidence and the Woman:[2] J. Clay Powers.
   { Trifles: Susan Glaspell.
8. Her Husband's Wife: A. E. Thomas.
9. Suppressed Desires: Susan Glaspell.
10. The Florist Shop:[1] Winifred Hawkridge.

165

1922–1923

1. CLARENCE: Booth Tarkington.
2. AMBUSH: Arthur Richman.
3. THE THINGS THAT COUNT: Lawrence Eyre.
4. THE TRUTH ABOUT BLAYDS: A. A. Milne.
5.[3] { THE MEDICINE SHOW: Stuart Walker.
       JUST NEIGHBORLY: Alexander Dean.
       MASTER PIERRE PATELIN: Anonymous.
6. THE RED ROBE: Eugene Brieux.
7. DULCY: George S. Kaufman and Marc Connelly.
8. THE DOVER ROAD: A. A. Milne.

1923–1924

1. WHY MARRY? Jesse Lynch Williams.
2. JANE CLEGG: St. John Ervine.
3. THE TORCHBEARERS: George Kelly.
4. ROMEO AND JULIET: William Shakespeare.
5. BELINDA: A. A. Milne.
6. A BILL OF DIVORCEMENT: Clemence Dane.
7. MARY THE THIRD: Rachel Crothers.
8. JUDGE LYNCH:[4] John William Rogers.

1924–1925

1. FASHION: Anna Cora Mowatt.
2. THE EMPEROR JONES: Eugene O'Neill.
3. PYGMALION: Bernard Shaw.
4. THE TRAGEDY OF NAN: John Masefield.
5. SEVENTEEN: Booth Tarkington.
6.[3] { SAVED: John William Rogers.
       IN THE SMOKIES: Norman Crowell.
       'TIL LIFE DO US PART: John William Rogers.
7. MR. PIM PASSES BY: A. A. Milne.
8. OUTWARD BOUND:[5] Sutton Vane.
9. THE NO 'COUNT BOY:[4] Paul Green.

1925–1926

1. WAPPIN' WHARF: Charles S. Brooks.
2. CANDIDA: Bernard Shaw.
3. OLD MAN MINICK: Edna Ferber and George S. Kaufman.
4. ANNA CHRISTIE: Eugene O'Neill.
5. DEAR BRUTUS: James M. Barrie.
6. JOHN FERGUSON: St. John Ervine.
7. THE YOUNGEST: Philip Barry.
8. EL CRISTO: [4] Margaret Larkin.

1926–1927

1. THE BEGGAR'S OPERA: John Gay.
2. MERTON OF THE MOVIES: George S. Kaufman and Marc Connelly.
3.[5]
   - A DANCE PANTOMIME: Ruth Laird and Frank Herring.
   - THE NATIVITY AND ADORATION CYCLE: from the Chester Mysteries.
   - WHY THE CHIMES RANG: Elizabeth McFadden.
4. HEDDA GABLER: Henrik Ibsen.
5. AREN'T WE ALL? Frederick Lonsdale.
6. BEYOND THE HORIZON: Eugene O'Neill.
7. RIP VAN WINKLE: Joseph Jefferson and Dion Boucicault.
8. MRS. PARTRIDGE PRESENTS: Mary Kennedy.

1927–1928

1. RIGHT YOU ARE (IF YOU THINK YOU ARE): Luigi Pirandello.
2. SUN UP: Lula Vollmer.
3. THE MONKEY'S PAW: [6] W. W. Jacobs and Louis N. Parker.
4. THE LITTLE STONE HOUSE: [6] George Calderon. (From the Russian.)
5. THE STEPMOTHER: [6] Arnold Bennett.
6. YOUNG WOODLEY: John Van Druten.

7. TWILIGHT SAINT: [6] Stark Young.
8. THE LAST OF MRS. CHEYNEY: Frederick Lonsdale.
9. THE SWAN: Ferenc Molnar.
10. THE GOOD HOPE: Herman Heijermans.
11. EXPRESSING WILLIE: Rachel Crothers.

1928–1929

1. WHAT EVERY WOMAN KNOWS: James M. Barrie.
2. LILIOM: Ferenc Molnar.
3. THE QUEEN'S HUSBAND: Robert E. Sherwood.
4. R.U.R.: Karel Capek.
5. ARMS AND THE MAN: Bernard Shaw.
6. THE CRADLE SONG: Martinez-Sierra.
7. THEY KNEW WHAT THEY WANTED: Sidney Howard.
8. LADY WINDERMERE'S FAN: Oscar Wilde.

1929–1930

1. ENTER MADAME: Gilda Varesi and Dolly Byrne.
2. THE ADDING MACHINE: Elmer Rice.
3. THE PLAY'S THE THING: Ferenc Molnar.
4. TEN NIGHTS IN A BARROOM: T. S. Arthur.
5. THE WILD DUCK: Henrik Ibsen.
6. THE ROYAL FAMILY: George S. Kaufman and Edna Ferber.
7. THE SILVER CORD: Sidney Howard.
8. THE DEVIL'S DISCIPLE: Bernard Shaw.
9. THE PERFECT ALIBI: A. A. Milne.
10. THE CRIMINAL CODE: Martin Flavin.
11. WEDDING BELLS: Salisbury Field.
12. HOLIDAY: Philip Barry.
13. ALICE IN WONDERLAND: Lewis Carroll.

1930–1931

1. BIRD IN HAND: John Drinkwater.
2. CAMILLE: Alexandre Dumas fils.
3. HOTEL UNIVERSE: Philip Barry.

4. { ANDROCLES AND THE LION: Bernard Shaw.
   { THE MAN WHO MARRIED A DUMB WIFE: Anatole France.
5. THE CONSTANT WIFE: Somerset Maugham.
6. THE DYBBUK: S. Ansky.
7. THE RACKET: Bartlett Cormack.
8. THE TORCHBEARERS: George Kelly.

1931–1932

1. THE SECOND MAN: S. N. Behrman.
2. SPREAD EAGLE: Charles S. Brooks and Walter B. Lister.
3. SAINT JOAN: Bernard Shaw.
4. SIX CHARACTERS IN SEARCH OF AN AUTHOR: Luigi Pirandello.
5. GREEN GROW THE LILACS: Lynn Riggs.
6. ONCE IN A LIFETIME: George S. Kaufman and Moss Hart.
7. LOYALTIES: John Galsworthy.
8. IN LOVE WITH LOVE: Vincent Lawrence.

1932–1933

1. BRIEF MOMENT: S. N. Behrman.
2. THERE'S ALWAYS JULIET: John Van Druten.
3. ROAM THOUGH I MAY:[2] John William Rogers.
4. SUCCESS STORY: John Howard Lawson.
5. CAESAR AND CLEOPATRA: Bernard Shaw.
6. THE YOUNG IDEA: Noel Coward.
7. THE HIGH ROAD: Frederick Lonsdale.
8. LITTLE THEATRE Varieties.
9. THE MARQUISE: Noel Coward.

1933–1934

1. BOTH YOUR HOUSES: Maxwell Anderson.
2. ON APPROVAL: Frederick Lonsdale.
3. THREE-CORNERED MOON: Gertrude Tonkonogy.
4. AMACO: Martin Flavin.
5. BIOGRAPHY: S. N. Behrman.

6. {A VILLAGE WOOING:[2] Bernard Shaw.
{THE MAN OF DESTINY: Bernard Shaw.
7. THE LOWER DEPTHS: Maxim Gorky.

1934–1935

1. ELIZABETH THE QUEEN: Maxwell Anderson.
2. EASY VIRTUE: Noel Coward.
3. THE LATE CHRISTOPHER BEAN: Sidney Howard.
4. THE DEVIL PASSES: Benn W. Levy.
5. DANGEROUS CORNER: J. B. Priestley.
6. YELLOW JACK: Sidney Howard.

1935–1936

1. RAIN FROM HEAVEN: S. N. Behrman.
2. {TILL THE DAY I DIE: Clifford Odets.
{WAITING FOR LEFTY: Clifford Odets.
3. POST ROAD: Wilbur Daniel Steele and Norma Mitchell.
4. THE DISTAFF SIDE: John Van Druten.
5. CANDLE LIGHT: Siegfried Geyer and P. G. Wodehouse.
6. BORNED IN TEXAS (ROADSIDE): Lynn Riggs.

1936–1937

1. PARNELL: Elsie Schauffler.
2. {DR. FAUSTUS: Christopher Marlowe.
{SQUARING THE CIRCLE: Valentin Katayev.
3. BLIND ALLEY: James Warwick.
4. NOAH: André Obey.
5. CAPTAIN BRASSBOUND'S CONVERSION: Bernard Shaw.
6. LOVE PASSES BY: Brothers Quintero.
7. NIGHT OF JANUARY 16: Ayn Rand.
8. CALL IT A DAY: Dodie Smith.
9. FIRST LADY: Katherine Dayton and George S. Kaufman.

1937–1938

1. THE WORLD WE LIVE IN (THE INSECT COMEDY): Karel Capek.

2. PRIDE AND PREJUDICE: Helen Jerome.
3. IDIOT'S DELIGHT: Robert E. Sherwood.
4. LYSISTRATA: Aristophanes.
5. STAGE DOOR: George S. Kaufman and Edna Ferber.
6. AN ENEMY OF THE PEOPLE: Henrik Ibsen.
7. EXCURSION: Victor Wolfson.
8. DEAD END: Sidney Kingsley.
9. THE CONCERT: Hermann Bahr.
10. ALICE IN WONDERLAND: Lewis Carroll.
11. THE BLUE BIRD: Maurice Maeterlinck.
12. BIG LAKE: Lynn Riggs.

1938–1939

1. TONIGHT AT 8:30: Noel Coward.
2. BROTHER RAT: John Monk, Jr. and Fred Finklehoff.
3. THE GHOST OF YANKEE DOODLE: Sidney Howard.
4. AUTUMN CROCUS: C. L. Anthony.
5. FLIGHT 21: Paul Baumer.
6. ARMS AND THE MAN: Bernard Shaw.
7. HOLY NIGHT: Martinez-Sierra.
8. ⎰ SNICKERTY-NICK: [7] Julia Ford.
   ⎱ THE AFFECTED YOUNG LADIES: [7] Molière.

1939–1940

1. ROOM SERVICE: John Murray and Allen Boretz.
2. OUR TOWN: Thornton Wilder.
3. ACCENT ON YOUTH: Samson Raphaelson.
4. JULIUS CAESAR: William Shakespeare.
5. SUSAN AND GOD: Rachel Crothers.
6. AH! WILDERNESS: Eugene O'Neill.

1940–1941

1. MARGIN FOR ERROR: Clare Boothe.
2. DOLLAR DOWN: [2] Margaret Sims.
3. NIGHT MUST FALL: Emlyn Williams.

4. WHERE THE DEAR ANTELOPE PLAY:[2] John William Rogers.

5. THE MALE ANIMAL: James Thurber and Elliot Nugent.

6. WE ARE BESIEGED:[2] Sam Acheson.

1941–1942

1. GEORGE WASHINGTON SLEPT HERE: George S. Kaufman and Moss Hart.

2. THUNDER ROCK: Robert Ardrey.

3. VINCENT VAN GOGH: Arnaud d'Usseau and Richard Collins.

4. MR. AND MRS. NORTH: Owen Davis.

5. SHADOW AND SUBSTANCE: Paul Vincent Carroll.

6. THE SNOW-MAIDEN: Alexander Ostrovsky (translated by David Russell, music by Rimsky-Korsakoff).

7. THE WOMEN: Clare Boothe.

8. THE GHOST TRAIN:[8] Arnold Ridley.

9. CRADLE-SNATCHERS:[8] R. G. Medcraft and Norma Mitchell.

1942–1943

1. THREE MEN ON A HORSE:[8] John Cecil Holm and George Abbott.

2. THE EVE OF SAINT MARK: Maxwell Anderson.

3. PETTICOAT FEVER:[8] Mark Reed.

4. THE TIME OF YOUR LIFE: William Saroyan.

5. KIND LADY: Edward Chodorov.

6. CANDIDA: Bernard Shaw.

[1] One-act play staged for the Community Chest.
[2] First performance.
[3] Triple bill of one-act plays.
[4] One-act play; Belasco Cup winner.
[5] Guest cast from leading Little Theatres in the United States.
[6] One-act play; Workshop production.
[7] Children's Theatre production.
[8] Army Camp shows.

Bibliography

ALLEN, FRANK LEWIS. *Only Yesterday*. New York: Harper and Bros., 1931.

ARVOLD, ALFRED G. *The Little Country Theatre*. New York: Macmillan Co., 1922.

BARKER, HARLEY GRANVILLE. *The Exemplary Theatre*. Boston: Little, Brown and Co., 1922.

———. *The Use of the Drama*. Princeton, N. J.: Princeton University Press, 1945.

BEARD, CHARLES A. and MARY R. *America in Midpassage*. New York: Macmillan Co., 1939.

BROWN, GILMOR and GARWOOD, ALICE. *General Principles of Play Direction*. New York, Samuel French, 1940.

CHENEY, SHELDON. *Stage Decoration*. New York: John Day Co., 1928.

———. *The Art Theatre*. New York: Alfred A. Knopf, 1917.

———. *The Theatre: 3000 Years of Drama, Acting and Stagecraft*. New York: Longmans, Green and Co., 1929.

CRAFTON, ALLEN. *Play Directing*. New York: Prentice-Hall Inc., 1938.

CRAFTON, ALLEN and ROGER, JESSICA. *The Complete Acted Play from Script to Final Curtain*. New York: F. S. Crofts and Co., 1943.

CRAIG, GORDON. *The Theatre—Advancing*. Boston: Little, Brown and Co., 1928.

CRUMP, LESLIE. *Directing for the Amateur Stage*. New York: Dodd Mead and Co., 1935.

DEAN, ALEXANDER. *Fundamentals of Play Directing*. New York: Farrar and Rinehart, 1941.

———. *Little Theatre Organization and Management*. New York: D. Appleton-Century Co., 1926.

DOLMAN, JOHN. *The Art of Play Production*. New York: Harper and Bros., 1928 (revised 1946).

173

DRUMMOND, A. M. *A Manual of Play Production*. Ithaca, N. Y.: The Author, 1930.

FERNALD, JOHN. *The Play Produced*. London: The Year Book Press, 1934.

FLANAGAN, HALLIE. *Arena: The Story of the Federal Theatre*. New York: Duell, Sloan and Pearce, 1940.

————. *Dynamo* (Vassar Experimental Theatre). New York: Duell, Sloan and Pearce, 1943.

GASSNER, JOHN and BARBER, PHILIP. *Producing the Play*. New York: The Dryden Press, 1941.

GILDER, ROSAMOND. *A Theatre Library*. New York: Theatre Arts, Inc., for National Theatre Conference, 1932.

HALSTEAD, WILLIAM PERDUE. *Stage Management for the Amateur Theatre*. New York: F. S. Crofts and Co., 1937.

HAYAKAWA, S. I. *Language in Action*. New York: Harcourt, Brace and Co., 1941.

HEFFNER, HUBERT C., SELDEN, SAMUEL and SELLMAN, HUNTON D. *Modern Theatre Practice*. New York: F. S. Crofts and Co., 1946.

HEWITT, BERNARD. *The Art and Craft of Play Production*. New York: J. P. Lippincott and Co., 1940.

HINSDELL, OLIVER. *Making the Little Theatre Pay*. New York: Samuel French, 1925.

HOPKINS, ARTHUR. *How's Your Second Act?* New York: Samuel French, 1931.

HOUGHTON, NORRIS. *Advance from Broadway: 1900 Miles of American Theatre*. New York: Harcourt, Brace and Co., 1941.

HUME, SAMUEL J. and FOSTER, LOIS M. *Theatre and School*. New York: Samuel French, 1933.

ISAACS, EDITH J. R., ed. *Theatre: Essays on the Arts of the Theatre*. Boston: Little, Brown and Co., 1927.

KROWS, ARTHUR E. *Equipment for Stage Production*. New York: D. Appleton and Co., 1928.

————. *Play Production in America*. New York: Henry Holt and Co., Inc., 1916.

MARKHAM, HAROLD. *The Amateur Theatrical Handbook*. London: Putnam and Sons, Ltd., 1927.

MACGOWAN, KENNETH. *Footlights Across America*. New York: Harcourt, Brace and Co., 1929.

MACKAY, CONSTANCE D'ARCY. *The Little Theatre in the U. S. A.*
New York: Henry Holt and Co., 1917.

McCLEERY, ALBERT and GLICK, CARL. *Curtains Going Up.* New
York and Chicago: Pitman Publishing Co., 1939.

MITCHELL, ROY E. *The School Theatre.* New York: Brentano's,
1925.

OMMANNEY, KATHERINE ANNE. *The Stage and School.* New York:
Harper and Bros., 1932.

PERRY, C. A. *The Work of the Little Theatres.* New York: Russell
Sage Foundation, 1933.

PLAYFAIR, NIGEL. *Hammersmith Hoy.* London: Faber and Faber,
1930.

PURDOM, C. B. *Producing Plays.* New York: E. P. Dutton and Co.,
1930.

ST. JOHN, CHRISTOPHER, ed. *Ellen Terry and Bernard Shaw: A
Correspondence.* New York: Putnam's Sons, 1932.

SHAW, GEORGE BERNARD. *The Art of Rehearsal.* New York: Samuel French, 1928.

SHAY, FRANK. *The Practical Theatre.* New York: D. Appleton Co.,
1926.

SIMONSON, LEE. *The Stage Is Set.* New York: Harcourt, Brace and
Co., 1932.

————. *Part of a Lifetime.* New York: Duell, Sloan and Pearce,
1943.

SMITH, MILTON. *The Book of Play Production.* New York: D. Appleton Co., 1927.

STRATTON, CLARENCE. *Producing in Little Theatres.* New York:
Henry Holt and Co., 1932.

THEATRE ARTS MONTHLY. *The Tributary Theatre* (annually, in
July issue). New York: Theatre Arts, Inc.

WALSER, FRANK LEWIS. *The Art of Conference.* New York:
Harper Bros., 1933.

WISE, CLAUDE M. *Dramatics for School and Community.* Cin-
cinnati: Stewart, Kidd and Co., 1923.

YOUNG, STARK. *Theatre Practice.* New York: Charles Scribner's
Sons, 1926.

————. *The Flower in Drama.* New York: Charles Scribner's Sons.
1923.

3 5282 00272 7009

Date Due